"An affecting memoir of life in small-town Kansas."

—*Kirkus Reviews*

"The son of a salvage yard owner-turned-farmer-turned-rancher, Robert Rebein grew up on ground that is hallowed in the American imagination. *Dragging Wyatt Earp* chips away at the myths encrusting Dodge City, offering instead a wry, bittersweet portrait of the New West. This memoir cracks wise about the experience of being a boy—watchful, jittery; full of high jinks, bravado and yearning—and about how we humans go about laying to heart the place we have to leave in order to love."

—Jennifer Brice, author of *Unlearning to Fly* and
The Last Settlers

" 'If the Old West was about blood and money,' Robert Rebein writes, 'the New West is about return.' Here prodigal Rebein returns to Dodge (a place most are in a proverbial hurry to get the hell out of) but also to his past, inhabiting it again like one of the farmhouses on the properties his father was forever buying. Charming, searching, and haunting all at once, this book makes me nostalgic for my own handful of years on the Great Plains."

—Bob Cowser, Jr., author of *Green Fields and Dream Season*

" 'Like the region's cattle, wheat, and corn, we'd been raised for export,' Robert Rebein writes of his Dodge City upbringing, but even though an expatriate, his heart, his mind, and his intellect were all formed under the stars of Ford County.

In this personal history, we also learn Western history, from Coronado to Custer to cowboys. We learn how art can be first manifested in an auto body shop, in a boy who shines chrome hubcaps to gold, and in a young man who reads Hardy's Tess in a grain truck between wheat harvest loads. Rebein is both homeboy and tourist as he visits his past, as well as the future: feedlots, rodeos, and casinos. As he deftly places himself in his 'home on the range,' he restores Kansas and the Great Plains to their rightful place in the American story."

—Thomas Fox Averill, author of *rode* and editor of *What Kansas Means to Me: Twentieth-Century Writers on the Sunflower State*

"Robert Rebein's *Dragging Wyatt Earp* is a profoundly American story. Rooted in a legendary town and a remarkable family, it is at once Rebein's unique narrative and one that belongs to all of us. Here are Earp and Custer, cowboys and Indians—the past that at once defies and defines us—alongside the remarkable yet ordinary people who, in our own time, make of everyday endurance a quiet form of heroism. *Dragging Wyatt Earp* captures the squalor and the splendor that lie at the heart of America as well as the powerful ties of family and community that enable us to live in such a place. Robert Rebein is a wonderful writer and *Dragging Wyatt Earp* is a beautiful book."

—Wayne Fields, author of *What the River Knows*

DRAGGING WYATT EARP

ROBERT REBEIN

DRAGGING WYATT EARP

A PERSONAL HISTORY OF DODGE CITY

SWALLOW PRESS   OHIO UNIVERSITY PRESS   ATHENS

Swallow Press
An imprint of Ohio University Press, Athens, Ohio 45701
www.ohioswallow.com

© 2013 by Ohio University Press
All rights reserved

To obtain permission to quote, reprint, or otherwise reproduce or distribute
material from Swallow Press / Ohio University Press publications, please contact
our rights and permissions department at (740) 593-1154
or (740) 593-4536 (fax).

Printed in the United States of America
Swallow Press / Ohio University Press books
are printed on acid-free paper ⊗ ™

20 19 18 17 16 15 14 13   5 4 3 2

Library of Congress Cataloging-in-Publication Data
Rebein, Robert, 1964–
 Dragging Wyatt Earp : a personal history of Dodge City / Robert Rebein.
    pages cm
 ISBN 978-0-8040-1142-6 (pbk. : alk. paper) — ISBN (invalid) 978-0-8040-4052-
5 (electronic)
 1. Rebein, Robert, 1964——Homes and haunts—Kansas—Dodge City. 2.
Dodge City (Kan.)—Social life and customs. 3. Rebein, Robert, 1964——
Childhood and youth. 4. Dodge City (Kan.)—History. I. Title.
 F689.D64R43 2013
 978.1'76—dc23
                          2012044512

To my parents, Bill and Patricia Rebein

Contents

Photographs follow page 89

Acknowledgments

Many people helped and encouraged me as I wrote this modest volume, and I would like to take a moment to thank a few of them.

My family: Bill and Patricia Rebein, David Rebein, Alan Rebein, Tom Rebein, Joe Rebein, Steve Rebein, Paul Rebein; my wife, Alyssa Chase, and my children, Ria and Jake Rebein; my mother-in-law, Andra Chase.

Friends and fellow writers: Mary Obropta, Anne Williams, Susan Shepherd, Karen Kovacik, Terry Kirts, Jacob Nichols, Joshua Green, Meagan Lacy, Christopher Schumerth, Kimberly Metzger, Joe Croker, Tim Cook, Benjamin Clay Jones, Nick Gillespie, Charlie Jones, Bryan Furuness.

Editors and former teachers: Kevin Haworth, David Gessner, Mark Lewandowski, Brendan Corcoran, Lauren Kessler, Randy Bates, Sarah Smarsh, Amber Lee, Lindsay Milgroom, Hillary Wentworth, Alys Culhane, Liz Dorn, Robert Stapleton, Mark Shechner, Bruce Jackson, Lynne Sharon Schwartz, Wayne Fields.

Dodge City people past and present: Marilyn Rebein, Kim and Beth Goodnight, John Rebein, Shane Bangerter, Kent Crouch, Tyrone Crouch, Bill Hommertzheim, Cathy Reeves, Jim Sherer, Charles and Laura Tague George, Pat George, Bob George, Trina Triplett Rausch, Regina Hardin Eubank, Heather Fraley Schultz, Gina McElgunn Tenbrink.

To all of you I owe my heartfelt thanks.

Several of the essays in this collection have appeared, in somewhat different form, in the following publications: "Return to Dodge City" in *The Cream City Review* (Fall 1994); "The Identity Factory" in *Inscape* (2010); "Dragging Wyatt Earp" in

Ecotone: Reimagining Place (Fall 2007); "The Greatest Game Country on Earth" in *Grasslands Review* (2009); "Sisyphus of the Plains" in *Redivider* (Fall 2010); "A Most Romantic Spot" in *Bayou* (2008); "The Search for Quivira" in *Umbrella Factory* (December 2010); "Horse Latitudes" in *Booth* (Summer 2012); "How to Ride a Bronc" in *Etude: New Voices in Literary Non-fiction* (Summer 2010).

Prologue

Christmas Eve 1990. I'm in a car on my way west across Kansas, the heart of it all, the prairie-bound stomach of the country, headed for a white-frame farmhouse where I know one light still burns in the kitchen. Outside, a cold, dry winter has set in. The Flint Hills are brown. Six states lay stretched out behind me. And I'm thinking, *Here comes full circle, here comes the loop the ropers say you rebuild every time it gets tangled. From the horse's back you rebuild it, hand over hand, loop upon loop, until all the rope is in.*

The road is dark, with just the white lines threading a path across the prairie. I squint my eyes, lean forward, switch back and forth between low and high beam, and for a moment it almost seems like the road itself is just a blurred projection thrown out by the headlights.

I see again the roughshod progression of my life, so many snapshots strung together like pearls: the early years in town, working with my father on the farm, school days, the time spent abroad, the coming back again. Returning home is like that. The future gets left behind, a piano dumped on a stark prairie. Suddenly you're left with nothing but your life and the past. You have returned. Full circle. Everything else is just a blur.

There is one memory I will always associate with my father. It is early winter, 1978 or 1979, and he is standing in his work clothes before the doorway of the Knoeber place, a ramshackle farmhouse, hatless, his legs thrown wide, motioning to me with the back of his hand in the rearview mirror of a wheat truck: *Back—and back—and back—and whoa!* Without pause, his gloved hand turns palm up and stops. I set the parking brake, check the mirror again, and he's already raking his index finger across his throat, a signal for me to kill the engine and join him inside. Another old farmhouse. Another relic from the age of one farmer for every square mile instead of one aging caretaker for every five. Like a lot of other contemporary farmers, my father acquired land the way some people acquire memories; and many times, the land came with a house, gratis.

Some of these places had been abandoned for years. Maybe an aging widow had lived there in the lingering aura of 1965, the year her husband died and she rented the land to neighbors. Or maybe the husband was the one who had survived, a widowed farmer who somewhere along the line stopped wiping his feet at the door, rebuilt carburetors at the kitchen table, and gradually let all housekeeping go to the dogs. Or maybe it was a long series of nobodies who stayed there—railroad men, pheasant hunters, bikers, what have you. The basements of such places would be filled to the floor joists with everything from prayer books to pornography: rusty knives, golf clubs, warped photographs and records, calendars and almanacs, canned vegetables grown murky in their ancient Kerr jars, bicycle parts, garden tools, children's books. In the basement of the Knoeber place, for example, we found three thousand Dr. Pepper bottles stacked neatly in crates. In the overgrown yard, a mountain of Alpo cans and their jagged, rusted lids. The mountain extended downward past ground level, where we found the dull, discarded can openers. At a deeper level, the bones of two medium-sized dogs. For years afterward, every time we mowed the grass, another of the phantom lids would emerge, sharpened and propelled through the air like some weapon in the martial arts.

All of these things my father took in stride as the not-so-heavy burden of his inheritance. Anything without immediate use we burned or hauled away. He liked to keep the earth turned, the pastures mowed, and the ditches sprayed with 2,4-D. Wichita pheasant hunters would drive by our fields and marvel at the absence of cover. Only later, after he traded farming for ranching, did he and my mother take to roaming country auctions and roadside antique stores. By then he'd bought a horse buggy from the Amish in Yoder, liked to drive out through his acres behind the steady clip of a pacer. This was the man who at one time had embraced every advancement in modern agriculture. The man who in his prime had nine center-pivot irrigation systems draining the local aquifer at the rate of seven or eight thousand gallons of water a minute, who drove cheap Japanese pickups because they got better mileage, who took his worn-out horses to the slaughterhouse instead of putting them out to pasture.

Over the years he'd grayed, softened. The fierceness with which he'd once looked upon his life was replaced with a kind of awe. On the day he finally bought the ranch he'd had his eye on for years, he took my mother to the top of its highest bluff. *Look down at that*, he said. *All my life I've wondered what Jesus must have been looking at when Satan tempted him the third time. Now I know. The land. All the kingdoms of the world.*

By the winter of 1990, Dodge City was again an open town. You could sense it driving in from the east. The population had grown by a third since I'd left, most of it made up of young men come north from Texas and Mexico to work in the newly built packing plants. Like the cowboys of old, they are mercurial and often well armed. Roughly a million cattle a year are slaughtered at Dodge City. The Roundup Rodeo, which headlines the annual Dodge City Days celebration, has grown from a small, local affair to one of the richest on the Professional Rodeo Cowboys Association circuit. It is as if the Old West, that brief period in the town's storied past, has returned, big as life in the twentieth century.

Of course the Old West always was about blood and money. The town got its start, after all, as a group of tents straddling a muddy lane, five easy miles from the army outpost to whose soldiers it sold whiskey, women, and the small hope of a world away from Indian fighting and the rolling monotony of the high plains. When the railroad arrived in 1872, the tents were replaced by false-fronted wooden shanties. Buffalo hunters, greased with blood, rolled into town aboard wagonloads of wooly black hides, the likes of which were already stacked ten and twenty feet high next to the depot. There's a picture of a man, Charles Rath, sitting atop a stack of forty thousand such hides that appears in all histories of Dodge. Behind him, just out of the picture, is the depot, and across from that is the Long Branch Saloon. Evidently there was something about a day spent in killing that required a shot of whiskey come nightfall; the founders of Dodge City understood this and built a big part of their business plan around it.

When the Indians were contained and the buffalo killed off, a new source of income, a second boom, rumbled on the southern horizon. Giant herds of Texas longhorns, banned by the bigger railroad towns to the east, began to replace the scalp-and-hide business as the town's chief bad smell and most recent reason-to-be. Like the soldiers and the buffalo hunters before them, the pimpled, adolescent cowboys who came north with the herds were bored, thirsty, and easily separated from their money. Hence the sharks—the professional gamblers, pimps, and hired guns—who also appeared, like horseflies on the stacked buffalo hides of old.

In the first year of its existence, Dodge City buried seventeen men, all of whom died "with their boots on." Probably three-quarters of its women were prostitutes, or "soiled doves," as the frontier papers called them; more than half of its buildings, saloons. Dubbed *The Queen of the Cowtowns* by its first class of merchant-citizens, the town went by a different name in the eastern papers: *The Wickedest Little City in the West*. Drive into town today and there's a sign that offers yet another moniker: *Dodge City, Kansas—Cowboy Capital of the World*.

It didn't last, of course. Even as the "better folk" in the town—the farmers, the merchants, and their wives—were busy crying out for the end of lawlessness, the boom, like all things, was ending of its own accord. In time, the false-fronted wooden shanties of old were replaced, first by brick buildings and finally by gleaming white grain elevators. These were what Truman Capote noticed above all else when he rolled into town to research *In Cold Blood*. Grain elevators rising like Greek temples on the plains. Prairie skyscrapers. Big white pencils busily erasing the Old West of yore.

Yet many would be the times when in the safety of their hard, honest work, the farmer-merchants of Dodge would look back with longing on a past their ancestors had deplored. They were helped along in their nostalgia by the Great Depression, several Hollywood films, and a radio and television drama that twisted the truth beyond recognition, making them the heroes and putting the town's name once again on the lips of strangers.

That was the first omen of things to come. The second was when the town, seeing money to be made, had a replica of old Front Street put up for the tourist trade, causing some to believe that this newly built facade was the *real* Front Street, that the past was not gone, and that the West still lived in the red brick streets of a little farming burg. They didn't realize that when the West came again it would not be here, but on the kill floors of Excel Corporation and National Beef.

Ironically, these modern packing plants were built five miles east of town, just west of where the old fort stood during Indian fighting days. It is here the herds come to, in trucks now instead of by hoof. It is here where the hides pile up, waiting to be turned into baseball gloves and patent leather shoes. And it is here where the young men arrive (young women, too), in beat-up cars with Texas plates, seeking work on a butcher's assembly line.

If the Old West was about blood and money, the New West is about return. Prodigal son comes home to save the ranch, discover his ancestry, spark an old flame. In the process, he finds himself, who he is in the here and now. As I pull into town, I note all of the changes like paragraphs on a page. The widened streets, the cattle trucks, the bars along Wyatt Earp Boulevard with names like Las Palmas, La Lampara, Nuestra Familia.

A New West has come to Old Dodge City, I think with a laugh. *Am I the only one who likes this one better?*

Of my six brothers, four became lawyers, one a day trader, and one a general contractor—not a farmer or rancher among us. If you're thinking this is a source of disappointment for our father, think again. From the first, he actively discouraged us from seeking a future in farming or ranching. Not that he had to try too hard. The truth was, most of us hated farming. We'd seen too many wheat fields ruined by hail or drought, too many years taken off the old man's life by work and worry. Ranching was just as bad—a babysitting job that never ended, cattle out at midnight or in a deadly winter storm. And yet, as happens to many who leave the farming life behind, there was something in all of us that felt lost, in exile, vaguely end-of-the-line. Sitting behind desks in Dodge City or Kansas City or Buffalo, New York, we might find ourselves, at odd moments, staring at summer fields still visible beyond the highway. In conversation with one another, we would lapse into the old way of talking. *Remember when you almost ran over me with the sweep plow? What were we—twelve or fourteen? Remember the time all the cattle got out in the blizzard? How cold it was?* With a mixture of self-regard and scorn, we'd look at our own children and remark how easy they had it, how soft they were.

To our father, we must have seemed more soft still. Born during the Great Depression to parents he never knew, he was saved from the orphanage by the Sisters of St. Joseph, who kept him in their hospital dormitory until he was adopted by a

German-Catholic farm family. His childhood consisted of long days of hard work, nights spent listening to radio reports of World War II. And yet, to hear him talk, these were days of glory and heaven. "We used to shovel wheat into the granary by hand," he'd say. "Of course, it was four dollars a bushel back then . . ."

Our mother, by contrast, grew up in the city with a mother and stepfather who knew nothing of farm life. Her biological father, it was said, had come from ranching people, but that was neither here nor there. Her parents divorced when she was still a baby, and she didn't meet the man until many years later, when she was married and had a family of her own. When asked about him today, all she will say is, "We were better off without him."

Of these things our parents never spoke. Family meant mostly what they had built on their own. Our childhood was designed to prove the past wrong, and in large part, it did just that. We were happy, prosperous, destined for bigger things. In our kitchen hung a painting of the family tree: a real tree, healthy and young, with a different branch for each of us and on each branch a child, his birthday, the color of his hair and eyes. As the family grew, so did the web of our belonging. The oldest paved the way for the youngest in a world alive to the sound of our name. At school it would be, "Ah, yes, I had your brother for math," or, "You know, your father went here as a boy," an aged nun smiling down on us as if she were somehow part of the family, too. Years later, I recall being in my parents' house over the holidays when a stranger, one of my older brother's friends, walked in the door. One of my nephews, Ben or Adam, ran forward and stopped the intruder in his tracks. "We're Rebeins," the boy said. "Who are you?" That is exactly how we were raised.

My younger brother and I didn't learn of our father's adoption until we were in college. At first, it didn't seem to touch our world. But as time went on, the questions grew. Who were we really, if not Germans? Later, when we discovered the truth about our mother's maiden name, we wondered again, *Who, then?* At such times, it helped to feel rooted in the land, to know that there was section after section in Ford County, Kansas, that had the family name printed across them in bold type.

The land.

All the kingdoms of the world.

We're Rebeins. Who are you?

Fourteen miles northeast of Dodge City is the ranch my parents bought in 1989 and named, in a moment of unintended irony, the Lazy R. The ranch house, built in the 1920s, is a repository for their collection of antiques, which includes a wind-up Victrola and a black, wood-burning stove of the kind that once heated the basement in my father's childhood home. Before they remodeled the place, it had been home to various down-on-their-luck renters and not a few squatters, at least one of whom lived on deer killed along Sawlog Creek and cooked over a spit in the living room fireplace.

On Christmas Day, my father and I ride out to the ranch in his white Ford pickup. I've been out of the country for the better part of three years, and he wants to show me what he has planned for the place. The previous owner and his tenants left behind the usual junk—rusted-out cars and tractors and farm implements of every vintage, to say nothing of old windmills and mile upon mile of petrified posts and brittle barbed wire.

"We'll take and move all this junk out of here and get the grass back in shape," my father tells me with his usual optimism. "I think we'll put the corrals over there, and eventually I want to build a new shop and machine shed and replace all of this old fence, but for now we'll take it a couple of miles a year."

He pauses, looks around. "You know, this place was really something at one time."

"It still is," I say.

He smiles. "Maybe someday you'll have a place just like it."

"Maybe."

"Thing about it is," he says, "when you do, you'll know it's yours."

The land, all the kingdoms of the world, stretches out before us as we drive away.

PART I
THE TOWN

House on Wheels

The house I grew up in was a sprawling brick affair with a four-car garage, a fenced-in patio, and wide lawns of fescue that stretched off on either side of a concrete driveway that more than one neighbor half-jokingly described as "a parking lot." It was an impressive house, to be sure, but also a little odd. That oddity had to do, at least in part, with the neighborhood where the house was located, which was full of much smaller, two- and three-bedroom bungalows compared to which our five-bedroom house looked like a bloated mansion. But even more than this, the essential strangeness of the house had to do with the fact that it was built piecemeal, with additions and other renovations coming along every three or four years, whenever my mother had managed to put money aside or my father happened to be seized by some new idea he would sketch on the back of an envelope before committing the entire family to its execution.

"Remodeling"—that's how my parents referred to these seasons of furious activity, which required the family to huddle, refugee-like, in some semifinished part of the house (usually the basement) while the parts undergoing renovation were sealed off with plastic sheeting or blankets tacked into place with framing nails. In some respects, the years of my childhood were filled with little else but these fantastical and interminable "remodeling projects"—or at least that's the way it felt to me at the time. With few exceptions, all of the work involved in these projects was done by my father and older brothers, although sometimes a too-curious neighbor who stopped by to remark on our progress would be pressed into service for an hour or two, maybe even an entire weekend. In this way, my father silenced any potential outcry against the use of power tools late at night or in the predawn hours of Saturday and Sunday mornings. To complain too loudly was to risk being swept up in the madness that defined and set us apart as a family.

The house I have described as a bloated mansion (and I can already hear both of my parents' objections to this description) began its life as a three-room shack without electricity or running water in the high wheat country twenty miles north of Dodge City. That's where it sat, in the corner of an enormous wheat field, when my uncle Harold bought it in the late 1940s. Of course, Harold being Harold, the house didn't remain that way for long. During the decade or so he and my aunt Marilyn lived there, they doubled its size, adding two new bedrooms and a kitchen, as well as electricity and modern plumbing. By the time my parents acquired the house in the late 1950s, it had the look and feel of your average single-story, three-bedroom, clapboard-sided farmhouse—nothing fancy, perhaps, but clean and serviceable enough. That's pretty much where things stood when I was brought home from Dodge City's St. Anthony's Hospital in the late summer of 1964.

Not long after this, in 1965 or 1966, my mother, who had grown up three hours away in Wichita, began to complain about the eighty-mile-a-day, round-trip commute she made on bad country roads taking my older brothers to and from Sacred Heart Cathedral School in Dodge City. As more than one neighbor pointed out, a bus would have picked the boys up and carried them the twenty miles to a public school on the north side of Dodge, but this my mother, a Catholic convert, would not hear of. So long as there was a God in heaven looking down on her, she was determined to remain blameless in His eyes in all matters relating to the exercise of her faith. If she had to drive eighty miles a day to accomplish that, then so be it. However, if she *didn't* have to make that terrible and wasteful drive, well then, all the better. As it happened, my father had reasons of his own to move to town; he and Harold had just bought a salvage yard on the south side of Dodge City, and running this business would soon be a part of my father's daily routine.

As always happened once my parents decided something, it wasn't long before they took definitive action. Surveying the available properties in a five-block radius of Sacred Heart, they settled on a red brick house my mother pronounced her "dream house." "Oh, how I loved that house!" she tells me now, thinking back past fifty years. "I loved everything about it—the yard, the porch, the fireplace, the kitchen and living room. I would lay awake at night, planning where I was going to put every piece of furniture I owned, and even some I didn't own. I couldn't sleep for thinking about it. That's how excited I was."

They made an offer on the dream house the same day they walked through it, and that offer was promptly accepted. However, a few days later, the seller called my father to say he had another, higher offer, and did my father care to match it?

Here my father paused ominously. "Another offer," he said. "I'm sorry, but I wasn't aware that this was an *auction*."

"Pardon?" the seller asked, confused and perhaps a little intimidated by my father's tone.

"I made you an offer, and you accepted," my father said. "We shook hands on the deal. Where I come from, that brings the bargaining part to a close."

"Ah, well, yes," the seller stammered. "But you see, now there's this *second* offer, and, well, it's considerably higher than yours . . ."

Here the story breaks into a couple of different variants. According to one version, at this point my father slammed the wall phone into its receiver and turned to my mother, who was standing in the doorway to the kitchen, a horrified look on her face. "Deal's off, Pat," he told her. "I'm sorry, but we're just going to have to figure out something else to do." According to another, more detailed version, the plot thickened a month or so after this, when the seller called back to inform my father that the second, higher offer had fallen through, and the house was on the market once again, and did my father care to make a repeat offer? At which point my father is said to have laughed and told the man exactly where he could put every last red brick of that so-called dream house. Even as a very small child, this was the version I liked best, and I refused to have the story told any other way.

Regardless of how or why it came to pass, in the fall of 1966, my father bought a pair of vacant lots on the north side of Dodge City where he dug and poured a basement of the same size and dimensions as the house in the country. When the base-ment was finished that spring, he hired a local mover to jack the house off its foundations, slide it onto a kind of massive cart, and drag the structure twenty miles cross-country to its new neighborhood in town. This was one of the few times in his life my father ever hired someone else to do a job he might have done himself just as easily, and he soon regretted the decision.

"I should have known something was wrong when I asked the guy what I had to get out of the house before the move," my father remembers, "and he told me not a thing, just leave it all right where it was. Clothes in the closets, dishes in the cabinets, lamps sitting on end tables. Well, you can imagine how that turned out . . ."

As the story goes, my mother and a friend were sitting in the house drinking a cup of Earl Grey tea when the mover showed up with a sledgehammer he used to knock the brick chimney away from the side of the house the way a lumberjack might fell a tree. "I looked at my friend and said, 'Well, I guess we'd better get out now,'" my mother remembers. "'This house is headed to town!'" But things did not go so smoothly. Halfway in, the mover cut a corner too close, taking out a stop sign and a row of country mailboxes. A little farther on, the addition my uncle Harold had built on the house began to break away. ("The back bedroom fell off the dolly" is how my mother puts it.) By the time the movers succeeded in shoring up the house and drag-ging it the rest of the way to town, it was clear to everyone that they were far from being able to lower it onto the newly poured basement. And so the house sat in a field next to the VFW Hall while my mother, six months pregnant, waited anxiously, and my father considered what his next move would be.

What happened next was vintage Bill Rebein. Instead of cutting his losses and getting us into the house as soon as possible, he decided to escalate the matter even further, tearing the plaster out of the original part of the house and replacing it with Sheetrock. And since he was already committed to doing that, why not go ahead and change the floor plan of the house, too, adding an entryway off the back of the house and converting what had been an upstairs bedroom into a dining room? Briefed on these plans in the basement of her father-in-law's house in the country, where half the family was staying while the other half was farmed out to various relatives and friends, my mother sighed exactly once and said, "I don't care what you do so long as I'm back in my own house before the baby comes. Those are my terms. Take them or leave them."

"Oh, we'll be in *long* before that," my father promised, his voice booming with confidence. "After all, it's not like we're tearing the *whole thing* down and starting from scratch, you know."

All the while this was going on, a much bigger remodeling project, dubbed Urban Renewal, was taking place a few blocks away in downtown Dodge City. Front Street, arguably the most famous city block in all of the Old West, was being ripped out to make room for off-street parking and the widening of Chestnut Street, soon to be renamed Wyatt Earp Boulevard. However, before the wrecking ball arrived to perform this misguided task, all kinds of materials culled from the condemned buildings of Front Street went up for sale. Naturally, my father, a salvage man to his core, was there to pick through the offerings. Among the items he carried away from the auction was a pool table taken from a saloon, hundreds of square feet of suspended ceiling tiles, and a 4-by-8-foot glass door that had once served as the front entrance to the Nevins Hardware store. These and other salvaged materials he stored in an old granary at the farm while the house was lifted onto its new basement and the work of tearing out the old plaster commenced.

"You'd not believe the dirt that was in the walls of that house," my father remembers, shaking his head. "We shoveled

it straight out the front door to use as topsoil in the yard—
that's how much of it there was. You have to remember—that
old house sat out there in the country, unprotected by trees or
anything else, through the worst years of the Dust Bowl."

After the new Sheetrock was in, the next step in the project
was to finish out the new floor plan, including the new entry at
the back of the house, where it was supposed we boys would do
the bulk of our coming and going. Here my father was seized by
an idea of such surpassing simplicity and brilliance he couldn't
believe no one had thought of it before. Why not use the big
glass door that had once opened and closed on the patrons of
Nevins Hardware as the house's back door? With the door's
quiet, self-closing technology in place, there would be no more
yelling at kids about slamming screens such as happened two
hundred times a day at the farm. Instead, all you'd hear would
be the quiet hiss of the door closing tightly on itself. Think of
all the money you'd save on heating and cooling bills. And if you
needed to look out the back of the house to see what the little
devils were up to, all you had to do was walk to the glass door
and look straight out. What could be easier or better than that?

While this work of my father's dragged on from one week
to the next, my mother's pregnancy dragged on, too. It was
her seventh pregnancy in a little under thirteen years of marriage, and with each one, the complications grew. The problem
was her Rh-negative blood, which could lead to all kinds of
potential problems when, as in this case, the baby's blood was
Rh-positive. By late May of that year, when she was thirty-four
weeks along, the family doctor who delivered all of us boys was
adamant that the time had come to induce labor and "get that
baby out."

"But we're not in the new house yet," my mother said.
"Can't we wait a little longer?"

"What's a little longer?" the doctor asked, eyebrows raised
doubtfully. "A couple of days? A week? Remember, this is Bill
Rebein we're talking about."

Here my mother paused, biting her lower lip. "Maybe

you're right," she said, laughing nervously. "Maybe it is time, after all."

And so it happened that my little brother, Paul, was born while the great Move to Town was still under way. He spent a week in neonatal intensive care, then joined the rest of us in the basement of my grandparents' farmhouse west of town. And still the work on the house dragged on—into its second and then its third month.

"We got very good at camping out down there," my mother remembers. "Soup heated up on a Coleman stove, baths taken at the end of a garden hose. That's just the way it was. Either you accepted it, or you risked going crazy. I had a little phrase I would repeat to myself, whenever some new delay or complication would arise. 'And this, too, shall pass,' I'd say. 'And this, too, shall pass.'"

I was three years old when the Move to Town took place, and unlike my older brothers, who ranged in age from five to thirteen, I have no memory of the time when my family lived far from town in the corner of a gigantic wheat field, surrounded on all sides by mile upon mile of flat, windblown prairie. To me, that whole period is a series of strange, black-and-white photographs featuring skinny, shirtless farm kids riding 1950s-era bicycles or playing baseball in the corner of some dusty, God-forsaken pasture. When I appear at all in these photos, I am the babe in arms, the infant in swaddling clothes whose bald head barely sticks out above the top of his stroller. Nothing about the scene, from the crew cuts my brothers habitually sported to the fact that the pictures themselves were in black and white, resembled any part of my Technicolor childhood. Examining the two eras side by side in family photo albums was like comparing pictures of the Beatles circa 1964 to pictures of the band in its late-1960s incarnations. That same, perplexing leap forward obtained.

Pictures of the house taken during the early years in town show a rectangular structure, twenty feet across the front and forty-eight feet long, with green-and-white aluminum awnings over the windows and a small, sun-splashed front porch covered in indoor/outdoor carpeting the same color and texture as 1970s-era Astroturf. Aside from the strange back door and the fact that it sat in the middle of two wide lots—one of just two homes on that side of the street, while on the other side there were six homes crammed into an equal space—the house didn't look all that different from other houses in the neighborhood. However, that would change soon enough.

Sometime during our first year in town, my brother Paul decided to ride his baby walker—one of those four-wheeled, legs-through-holes, baby runabouts that have since been banned worldwide—down an unfinished flight of stairs leading to an uncarpeted expanse of raw concrete. When he reached the bottom, the walker slammed forward, and Paul cracked his head on the concrete floor with what has always been described to me as "a sickening thud." (This is how we discuss the event in my family, our sentences always beginning with Paul himself or else in the passive voice—*The door was left open*—so that all question of *how* this could have happened, or *who* could have left the door ajar, remain unasked.) In the aftermath of this terrible event, Paul was rushed to a small hospital in the middle of Dodge City and from there to a larger one three hours away in Wichita, where things got so bad for so long that my mother removed herself to the hospital chapel, where she remained on her knees, refusing to budge or even to talk, until news of a miracle was brought to her. Only Patricia Rebein and God Himself know what promises were made in that dark little chapel. However, they must have been sufficient, for against all odds, Paul pulled through with no permanent damage to his brain or any other part of him.

"It was a miracle, all right," my mother insists to this day. "All of the doctors and nurses agreed. They had never seen a situation that bad turn around that completely. Think about that the next time you need God's help."

Soon after this my father moved the stairs from the center of the house to the back, between the bathroom and the big glass door, so that now the stairs did not descend in a single flight but instead turned twice on the way down. They were covered as well in a thick shag carpet, such that a newborn might have tumbled down them without coming to any harm. Indeed, in the course of our childhood in the house, Paul and I used to trip or hurl each other down these stairs on a regular basis. However, they were so padded and safe, the effort was mostly wasted.

This moving of the stairs signaled the beginning of a larger remodeling project that soon saw the entire basement finished. When I asked my father, years later, what had guided his thinking in finishing the basement, he paused a moment, then replied, "Well, I had all those materials from Urban Renewal I wanted to use. The other part of the plan was to make the basement nice enough that you kids would stay down there and leave the upstairs to your mother and me."

He succeeded in both of these objectives. The new basement's wood paneling, ceiling tiles, door to the outside, and the pool table that was its most prominent and (in my eyes) most important feature had all enjoyed previous lives on Front Street in the years before the demolition, and there was no question the basement was an attractive place to hang out. More than half the square footage was given over to a carpeted TV room and an adjoining rec room housing the pool table and the family's new 8-track tape player. On the other side of the rec room were two dorm-like bedrooms, one green and one red, each featuring bunk beds along with built-in cabinets and desks. Rounding out the floor plan at the base of the stairs was a small bathroom with a tiled shower and the aforementioned door to the outside, a feature I came to appreciate fully only during my teenage years, when the ability to sneak in and out of the house without my parents knowing became such an all-important thing.

Once finished, the basement was ruled over by my older brothers, who soon instituted many arcane and (to my eyes) arbitrary rules concerning it. The first rule was that anytime an older brother wanted the use of a chair or any other piece of furniture being used by a younger brother, all the older brother had to do was to say the words "Pass down," and the younger brother was required to move at once. As you might expect in a family of seven boys, the free exercise of this law created many a musical chairs–like moment, as the oldest in the family kicked the next oldest out of his chair or couch, and that brother responded by invoking the pass down rule on the brother just beneath him in age, and so on, until finally all of the furniture in the room was occupied and those of us at the bottom of the pecking order had to lie on the carpeted floor to watch TV. Similar rules concerned the selection of TV shows (the oldest brother in the room always decided what we would watch), what music could be played on the 8-track and at what volume, and, most devastating to me, who was allowed to use the pool table.

"The felt on this table is brand new," one of my brothers intoned. "Do you think we want you ripping it up, or spilling juice on it, or anything like that?"

Needless to say, I ignored the rule regarding the pool table every chance I got, dragging a chair next to the table to stand on while I practiced my shots. My one desire in life was to become a billiards expert on par with my heroes Minnesota Fats and Willie Mosconi, who later took part in the legendary $15,000 "Great Pool Shoot-Out" announced by Howard Cosell on ABC's *Wide World of Sports*. However, short of this lofty goal, I would settle for beating any of my older brothers at a game of eight ball. I had noticed that as soon as one of my brothers got old enough to play in pool halls like the Golden Ace downtown or Duffy's in South Dodge, they quickly lost all interest in our table, and this was a weakness I planned to exploit. Finally, I got good enough to beat the next brother above me, Steve, and I began to set my sights even higher. However, I was disappointed to find that none of my brothers older than Steve would play me.

"You're all scared," I taunted them.

"That's not why," my brother Tom said with a laugh.

"Why then?"

"You'll find out, one of these days."

"Yeah, sure," I replied, thoroughly disgusted.

However, it turned out he was right after all. I did find out. As soon as I was old enough, I headed downtown and sneaked into the Golden Cue, where I challenged a middle-aged feedlot cowboy to a game of eight ball.

"How much you want to bet?" the cowboy asked.

"I don't know," I said. "How much do you want to bet?"

"How about five dollars?"

This was far more than I had been expecting, but I had the money on me, and by now it was impossible to back down. "You're on," I said.

Nothing about the table on which we played felt remotely like our table. The ball rolled much more slowly, and the action off the cue ball felt different, too. None of my trick shots—or even my regular shots—worked. After taking a licking in that game and one more, I headed home, tail between my legs, and found my brother Tom in the TV room, eating popcorn and watching a rerun of *Hawaii Five-O.*

"What's the deal with the pool table?" I asked.

"You've been playing at Duffy's, haven't you?" he observed with a smirk.

"The Golden Cue."

"And let me guess," Tom said, smiling broadly. "The table felt a little *different*."

"That's right. Why?"

Here Tom paused, obviously savoring the moment. "The tops on those tables are *granite*, fool."

"And our table?" I asked.

"Plywood."

"Plywood! What the hell! *Why?*"

"The top was broken when Dad bought it," Tom answered, shrugging. "That shit's expensive, so instead of granite, we used plywood and then had the whole thing covered with new felt so no one would notice."

Why do we have to be so different from everyone else? I remember wondering. As always, no answer to this important question was forthcoming.

I had just started school at Sacred Heart Cathedral when my parents decided it was high time to remodel the upstairs of the house. The decision was made over dinner one Friday night, and by Saturday afternoon, my father and older brothers had ripped the kitchen cabinets off the wall and tossed them unceremoniously into the front yard. The violence and finality of the action shocked me deeply. It was as if some kind of madness had come over these people I thought I knew, and they were behaving now as men possessed—as zombies or something worse, not to be trusted. I remember sitting on my bicycle in the middle of Cedar Street, which was then little more than a dirt road, watching the chaos and destruction unfold. First the cabinets flew out the side door, then the sink, followed by huge chunks of linoleum flooring that sailed through the air like wounded Frisbees. Then one of my brothers—I think it was Alan, the second oldest—came outside, sledgehammer in hand, and started to break apart the wooden porch on the north side of the house.

"What are you doing?" I asked.

"Dad said to," he answered in his zombie way. "We're gonna get rid of this whole doorway and expand this side of the house into the yard and make a sitting room for Mom."

"A sitting room?" I asked. "What's that?"

"I don't know," Alan replied. "But that's what Dad is calling it, so I guess that's what it's going to be."

Unlike the Move to Town and the finishing of the basement, neither of which I was old enough to remember in any detail, this round of remodeling was something I experienced directly, the way refugees in a war-torn country experience war. It was my turn now to understand what it meant to "camp" in the basement, sleeping on fold-out cots and cooking dinners of macaroni and cheese on a Coleman stove set up next to the pool table. For months, while the work dragged on and on, and ideas multiplied like flies, the family lived in a strange, almost surreal state in which everything that had once seemed "normal" was turned on its head, and even the strangest of circumstances provoked little more than a tired yawn. Was it "normal" to take your bath in a plastic baby pool, to think of a Styrofoam cooler as "the fridge," to eat Campbell's Chicken Noodle Soup over rice for fifteen days in a row? Well, who was to say it wasn't normal when clearly it was the only reality going?

And so the zombies continued with their dubious enterprise, fitting the work in on evenings and weekends and holidays such as Thanksgiving and New Year's. Watching the work take place, all I could do was shake my head and whisper my mother's old mantra under my breath, so no one else could hear, "And this, too, shall pass. And this, too, shall pass."

It did pass. And in time life went back to "normal" again. However, having experienced life as a refugee, I no longer trusted the whole idea of normalcy. Deep down, I knew that the zombies could reappear at any moment, and when that happened, the world as I knew it would be laid to waste as if a flood or a tornado had raged through the neighborhood.

The older I got, the more adept I became at forecasting the squall on the horizon that in time would grow into a full-blown storm of remodeling. Usually it began in this way. My mother, whom I was beginning to recognize as a co-instigator of the madness, rather than a co-victim, would express in passing some dissatisfaction with the house as currently configured. The bathroom was too small or in the wrong part of the house; whenever it rained, water ran down the basement steps, flooding the laundry room; the front room lacked a fireplace, and wouldn't it be grand to sit before a crackling fire, glass of wine in hand, kids exiled to the basement where they belonged? Hearing this, my father would remain quiet for a long time, his Rebein jaw thrust out before him. At first I thought this look was because he was mad at her; only later did I learn that the silence was a sign that the wheels in his mind had begun to turn, seeking answers to these riddles his mate had posed. Not long after the comments were made, the two of them would move on to the next inevitable stage in their process—driving around town to "look at houses." How I hated this ritual! Invariably the houses they looked at were in upscale neighborhoods like the one surrounding the country club golf course, a part of town universally derided as Snob Hill.

"There's no harm in looking," my mother would say at the beginning of one of these interminable expeditions.

"No, looking is free," my father would agree. "It's buying that's expensive."

Sitting in the backseat of the family Buick, a car I considered not nearly nice enough to be driving down these particular streets, I would try to predict the future by paying attention to which houses my parents looked at and what they said about them. It wasn't particularly hard.

MOM [*pointing to a two-story Tudor with a massive front lawn*]: Oh, I like that one, Bill.

DAD: The roof doesn't have enough overhang. [*Nodding at a single-story brick ranch with an open ceiling and massive windows across the front*]: What do you think of that one over there? Now that's a house.

MOM: Nice. But what do you suppose a house like that costs?

DAD [*shrugging*]: A lot. What do you think of that color of brick?

MOM: I like it. A lot.

DAD: So do I. See the way the chimney rises up on that side of the house . . .

Having heard this much, I knew it was just a matter of time before my father grabbed some piece of unopened mail and used the back of it to draw a rough sketch of his latest home improvement idea. *But was that really so bad?* I found myself wondering, as time went on. While part of me blamed both my parents for continually pulling the carpet out from under my childhood, another part of me was beginning to look at them with something like awe, maybe even admiration. *They're crazy as loons,* I'd think to myself. *But they certainly do know what they want, and they aren't shy about going after it.*

The biggest of my parents' "remodeling projects" stretched across several years in the late 1970s, when I was twelve or thirteen years old, and my oldest brother David was in law school at the University of Kansas. After years of talking about it, my parents were going to remodel the house's exterior, adding a shake shingle roof, a fireplace, and an exterior of new red brick. In essence, they were going to remake the house in the image of one of those sprawling ranches on Snob Hill they were always driving past and admiring. Of course, being Rebeins, they had their own way of going about this, one that only someone who knew their history and tendencies could have predicted.

During World War II, which coincided roughly with the later years of my father's childhood, Dodge City was a veritable hive of military activity, particularly as regarded the testing of aircraft and the training of pilots. Shortly after Pearl Harbor, an army air base home to some forty thousand people was thrown up in wheat fields west of town. There were massive airplane hangars, hundreds of smaller Quonset huts, and row upon row of temporary barracks heated by tall chimneys of red brick. In the years after the war, however, the old air base quickly fell into disrepair. Finally it was closed altogether, the barracks torn down, the Quonset huts and other usable buildings dragged off to nearby farms and ranches to serve as machine shops or cowsheds. Grass grew up in the cracks in the old runways, the old brick chimneys fell to the ground, and what remained of the place was turned into a feedlot for finishing cattle. My father had grown up less than a mile from the old air base and was intimately familiar with every part of it. However, the massive old hangars and the majestic runways and even the utilitarian Quonset huts were not what drew his attention. No, what stoked his desire and got his imagination

going was the thought of all those fallen-down barracks chimneys. All that brick just sitting there on the prairie waiting for
someone with the desire and initiative to imagine a use for it!
All that brick *for free!*

I remember the Saturday this desire of my father's was
translated into action. Two or three of my brothers and I were
loaded into the back of my father's snub-nosed 1969 Dodge
pickup and driven out to the old air base. There we were issued
tools and instructed to stand by and watch carefully as my father demonstrated the process we were to use in recycling the
bricks for use on our house.

"First you find a cluster of three or four bricks that have already fallen from the chimney," the old man told us, digging in
the weeds until he came up with a representative chunk. "Then you
carefully tap at the mortar between the bricks with your hammer
and chisel until you get them separated from each other. Finally
you chip away at the remaining mortar until . . ." But here, in
the final part of his demonstration, the brick he was cleaning
broke in half in his hands. "Well, you get the idea," he said,
tossing the broken brick back into the weeds and wiping the
mortar dust from his hands. "As you get the bricks cleaned, just
stack them in groups of a hundred or so, and we'll load them in
the pickup when I come back to get you."

And with that, he drove off, leaving us to our work. I can't
recall how much we were to be paid for this job—a couple of
cents a brick, I think. I know it was enough that I was vaguely
excited by the prospect of making the money to buy whatever
toy I had on my wish list in those days. However, this initial
enthusiasm soon wore off, as brick after brick broke in half
or disintegrated altogether in my chapped, red fingers. That
old army cement was just too tough and clingy, the bricks
too porous and fragile. In the four or five hours before my father returned to take us home for lunch that Saturday, I think
my brother Steve and I managed to clean all of three or four
bricks. The rest we had to toss back into the weeds from which
we had gathered them, and soon enough the hurling of these

bricks because the day's chief activity, complete with side bets on accuracy, and so on. My brother Joe concentrated much harder on the work but did no better. In any case, the sight of our tiny stack of cleaned bricks must have been all the old man needed to abandon all thought of cleaning enough bricks to cover our house, because we never returned to the air base to clean another brick after that day—indeed, we didn't even bother to take the bricks we had already cleaned home with us. For all I know, they're still sitting out there today on the broken tarmac, waiting for sun and rain to pound them back into the ground from which they came.

Despite this initial setback, the idea of bricking the house on Cedar went ahead as planned. I vividly recall the day the pallets of new bricks were off-loaded into our front yard, creating yet another of those No-Looking-Back moments, like the time my father told the seller of the "dream house" what he could do with it, or the time he and my brothers knocked a hole in the side of the house and began to throw cabinets out of it. *I guess it's really going to happen,* I thought, bracing myself for what I knew would be a difficult period of transition and toil. Was I myself becoming one of the zombies? I wondered. Yes and no, I decided. For even as I pulled on gloves and began moving the bricks to where the bricklayers could reach them, another part of me was already repeating the familiar words, "And this, too, shall pass. And this, too, shall pass."

It was around this time of heady activity on the exterior of the house that my brother David brought one of his law school friends home to spend Thanksgiving with us. I believe the guy was from out of state and had no one else to spend the holiday with. He probably imagined the weekend would be a good break from the toil of law school, a time to kick back, stuff himself with turkey, and watch some football on TV. What he got instead is a subject of amusement in my family even to this day. For no sooner had the poor devil been introduced to the family that Wednesday evening than a trenching spade was thrust into his hand and he had to pitch in, along with the rest of us, and help to dig footings for the new brick siding. After all, that's what evenings and weekends and holidays were for when a remodeling project was under way, and the work went on not just for an hour or two but for the entire weekend, including Thanksgiving Day.

"The poor bastard," one of us will say, remembering those days. "He didn't know what he was getting into. He thought we'd surely quit when it got dark. Imagine how shocked he must have been when Dad came out of the house with those floodlights, and we kept right on digging past ten o'clock."

Similar scenes played themselves out across the next couple of years, as a new roof of shake shingles was put on, the afore-mentioned patio was added, and, finally, the house's four-car garage was built. In many ways, this final project was my father's masterpiece. I was old enough by then to see how he went about it, and like everyone else who witnessed the process, I was both amused and amazed. First the foundations were dug and the footings were poured, followed by the floor of the garage and the driveway. When that was done, we set about building the rafters, stacking each new rafter we built atop the others on the patio.

"What about the walls?" a curious neighbor asked. "Ain't you gonna have walls on this gigantic thing?"

"Sure," my father answered. "I already have some ready and waiting."

"You already have some *walls?*" the man asked, his eyes bugging a little.

"Sure, at the farm," my father said. "I've got all the walls I need out there."

I remember standing there in my carpenter's apron, try-ing to visualize what my father was talking about. From what I could remember about the place, the old farmstead was little more than an abandoned basement, a rusted-out swing set, and a couple of rows of dying elm trees. Where these "walls" were coming from, I could not imagine.

I found out the very next weekend, when we pulled into the gravel driveway of the old farmstead twenty miles from town, and there at the very back of the property was an old, tin-sided government granary I had all but forgotten about.

"There are those walls I was telling you about," my father said to our dubious neighbor, who had accompanied us on the errand. "Pull that tin off and lift the roof, and those walls will come apart in sections, just like they were designed to do when the government put them up years ago."

"Well, I'll be damned," the neighbor said, a weak smile animating his face.

This time, everything came off just the way the old man said it would. Within a couple of hours of arriving, we were hauling our first load of walls to town. As we arrived with each load, a second crew got busy putting them up. It was like one of those Amish barn raisings, the massive garage seeming to grow out of thin air over the course of a single day, the walls rising first, followed by the rafters, followed by precut sheets of plywood we nailed into place before rolling out the tar paper and hammering on the shingles. That evening, we all stood around in the shadow of the thing we had built, drinking iced tea or beer and marveling at all we had witnessed and participated in that day.

When the house on Cedar was finally completed to my parents' satisfaction, it boasted five bedrooms, two bathrooms, and a white-carpeted living room with a stone fireplace separated from the rest of the house by French doors. By then, several of my brothers were skilled carpenters; one of them, Tom, had even gone into business for himself. The work they did on that house was professional grade, and yet, no sooner was it definitively finished, during my first year away at college, than my parents sold it and moved into the three-bedroom farmhouse west of town that my father had grown up in. I remember how shocked I was when my mother called and told me about these developments.

"You're selling the house?" I asked. "What on earth for?"

"It's part of a land deal," my mother said, sighing. "But the truth is, it's too big for us now anyway, with just your dad and me and your brother Paul left."

"Too big?" I asked. "Or too finished?"

Here my mother allowed herself a tiny laugh. "Ah, well, you know your father. He likes to have a project."

"Really? Just him?"

Another laugh.

That was two houses and twenty-five years ago. Although my parents are in their late seventies now and have lived in their current home on Snob Hill for only eighteen months, already I have noticed them looking around the place, commenting on what my father likes to call "the possibilities."

Hide the envelopes.

In the Land of Crashed Cars
and Junkyard Dogs

When I was a boy growing up in western Kansas, my father and his older brother, Harold, owned an auto body salvage yard in the sand hills south of Dodge City. The place was called B & B Auto Parts, or, more simply, B & B. That was the name of the business when they bought it in 1966, and that's the name it retains to this day, long after they sold it and my father returned to full-time farming and ranching. I remember, as a very small boy, asking my mother what the name stood for and why they never bothered to change it. "*I* don't know," she answered, continuing whatever chore she was doing at the time. "A, B, C—what does it matter? It's *just* a junkyard." Of course, she was right about that; my father himself would have agreed. And yet, to me, perhaps because of the age I was when I experienced it, the salvage yard was so much more than that. As Ishmael says of the whaling ships on which he grew to manhood, the salvage yard, with its forty-odd acres of mangled cars and trucks, was my Harvard and my Yale.

I was five or six years old when I started spending a lot of time at the salvage yard. I don't know how or why this came to pass, but I have my suspicions. From my earliest days, I was a handful—a hyperactive motor mouth prone to accidents and mischief of a more or less mindless sort. From the moment I woke up until I dropped to sleep from exhaustion seventeen or eighteen hours later, I was constantly on the go, constantly "causing a racket" and "failing to listen," constantly "into something." Today, kids such as I was get a dose of Ritalin. But I was lucky. The only solution that offered itself in my case was to send me to work along with my father and older brothers.

Of course, I use the phrase *to work* in only the loosest of senses. While most of my older brothers were given jobs as apprentice welders or body men or were at least required to push a broom every once in a while, I was allowed to roam free across the entire expanse of the salvage yard so long as I didn't maim myself or distract anyone else from his work. In this way, I came to know the different territories that made up the salvage yard, as well as the rogue's gallery of men who ruled over them.

The nerve center of the place was the concrete-floored front office with its long counter littered with coffee cups, overflowing ashtrays, dog-eared lists of inventory. Here parts men took orders from the public and added their voices to a static-ridden frequency on which their colleagues from across the West and Midwest carried on a nonstop conversation. *Guys, this is Bob at Apex in Tulsa still looking for that bumper, hood, and grill for a 1972 Buick Skylark. . . .* The Front was the only part of the salvage yard that was air conditioned or heated in any conventional sense (the body and machine shops made do with jerry-rigged box fans and fifty-gallon drums converted into wood-burning stoves). It was where customers waited, gossiping and smoking, lounging about on bucket seats culled from wrecks. Most importantly to me, though, the Front was where the candy and pop machines were. How I loved to scavenge coins from under the seats of wrecked cars and then feed them, one by one, into the rows of globe-headed machines containing jelly beans, gumballs, salted cashews, Boston baked beans, Red Hots, regular and peanut M&M's! This was my first real experience of the world of "getting and spending," as Wordsworth had it, and how sweet it was!

Snack and drink in hand, I'd sit, legs dangling from one of the old car seats, and wait for something interesting to happen. It never took long. Someone was always arguing, telling an off-color joke, showing off a new gun or knife he'd just bought or otherwise "come into." At first the parts guys, conscious of my presence, would nod toward me and quickly change the subject whenever someone ventured into R- or X-rated territory.

Gradually, however, they forgot about me and went on with their business uncensored. Many an old-time country song could be fashioned out of the words and deeds of the men who turned up at the salvage yard looking to coax a few more miles out of their battered Chevys and Fords. After a while, it began to seem to me that every story worth telling involved, as if by prescription, an angry woman, a bout of drinking, a fistfight, and a night spent in the city or county jail.

PARTS MAN 1: Bob! Ain't seen you in a coon's age. How the hell is it hanging?

BOB [smoking, looking a little haggard and hangdog]: Not so good. You heard the old lady threw me out on my ass, right?

PM 1: No! Why'd she go and do a thing like that?

BOB: Be damned if I know.

PARTS MAN 2 [chuckling, taking a long drag of his cigarette and letting the smoke escape his lungs along with the words]: Didn't have anything to do with you getting drunk and driving that Jeep of yours into that culvert off Comanche Street, did it?

BOB [sheepishly]: Well, yeah. But can you believe the bitch wouldn't even bail me out? I had to ask her cousin to do it!

PM 1 [winking at PM 2]: Which cousin would that be?

BOB [smiling faintly, as if reliving it all over]: I think you know the one I'm talking about. Young and long-legged . . .

PM 2: Well, now. I do believe this picture is starting to come into focus . . .

Like bartenders and other people who deal with the public all day, the parts men could be gregarious, gruff, sympathetic, or downright mean, depending on what the situation appeared to call for. For this reason, I didn't like them very much. Parts men were a little *too* slick, a little too shifty and hard to read. I hated it when they would treat a customer nice—*We'll be seeing you, Duane, take care now, you hear?*—and then start in laughing as soon as he was safely out the door. *That sumbitch gets any fatter he's gonna need a goddamn mirror just to see his own pecker ha ha ha . . .*

The Front was the place I first encountered the words *fuck, cunt,* and *cocksucker,* to say nothing of such tame elocutions as *shit, goddamn,* and *sonofabitch*. I remember once, having just overheard a sustained streak of animated cussing, I wandered out to the gravel parking lot and began to reenact the scene in a loud voice.

"And then I told that COCKSUCKER that if he didn't stop FUCKING with me I was gonna rip his MOTHERFUCKING head off and take a SHIT down his neck . . ."

Even as I said the words, I could hear the door to the Front swing open behind me, and who did I see when I turned around but my father in his blue uniform, black eyes boring into me.

"What did you just say?" he asked.

"Nothing," I answered.

"It didn't sound like nothing."

I hung my head a little, afraid to lie.

"What would your mother think if she heard you talking like that?"

"She wouldn't like it," I said.

"Have you ever heard *me* talk like that?"

"No."

"Well, all right then. I better not hear you. Understand?"

And with that he walked away, shaking his head in that exasperated way he had, as if to comment on how amazingly stupid the world had become sometime while he wasn't paying attention to it.

After the Front, my favorite part of the salvage yard was a long corridor that ran between the engine and body shops—a massive, Willy Wonka–like space filled with nothing but row upon row of chrome hubcaps. Hung on huge racks and lit up by columns of fluorescent lights, these hubcaps gleamed for me like the very gold of Cibola. Ford, Chevrolet, Pontiac, Buick, Oldsmobile, Chrysler . . . every American make and model was represented. I loved to sit against the wall opposite the hubcaps and cast my eyes over them until one in particular drew my attention, at which point I would rise, climb the racks, and bring the hubcap down to inspect it. My favorites were the vintage chrome hubcaps favored by Chevrolet in the 1950s and '60s. How sleek and perfect they were! Sitting on the ground, hubcap in my lap, my reflection bouncing mirror-like back to me, I could easily imagine the cap was. . . . a flying saucer . . . a cymbal on a drum set . . . a discus I was about to hurl in a bid to win the Olympics . . .

One day, as I lay on the floor amid a pile of caps, playing some game that existed only in my head, one of the parts men walked by and dropped a red shop rag in my lap.

"If you're gonna drag those sumbitches down, you might as well shine them up," he said.

I fell to this work without complaint or expectation of pay. Soon I created a special row on the racks just for the caps I had polished to an especially high luster. This was my hoard of gold, my kingdom of chrome.

Then one day I returned to my stash and found that my favorite hubcap of all was gone. I stood there, staring at the place on the rack it had occupied only the day before. Then, as the reality of the situation sank in, I rushed into the Front and demanded an explanation.

"That dog dish Chevy cap?" one of the parts men, a gruff, bear-like man named Kenny or Doug, said absently. "Sold it yesterday."

"You *sold* my hubcap?" I asked, astonished and appalled.

"Well, what did you *think* we did around here?" Kenny asked, laughing. "Play with ourselves?"

Only when he noticed the tears running down my cheeks did the man stop teasing me. "Hey, I'll tell you what," he said, reaching into the front pocket of his jeans. "How about I buy the cap from you for a nickel?"

"To hell with your nickel!" I spat, turning and running away from there until my lungs burned and my legs ached. After that, I would have nothing at all to do with Kenny. He and

I were enemies, even if he, in his gruff bearness, was oblivious to the fact.

Beyond the corridor where the hubcaps were stored was a large warehouse lined with heavy racks built to store engines, rear ends, transmissions, and large body parts like fenders and hoods. Hanging from each part was a tag with the wreck's year, make, and model scrawled in bright yellow paint—"1969 GTO," "1972 Gran Torino," "1974 Nova." As a young boy, I was fascinated by the names of these cars. I loved to say them out loud, feel the sound of them rolling off my tongue as I wandered the dimly lit rows of the warehouse, dodging the forklift that always seemed to appear out of nowhere, bearing down on me like some evil robot in a science fiction tale.

The parts themselves I found to be eerie and disturbing. Maybe it was the way they hung from their hooks like executed criminals. Or the way each figured as an orphan of sorts, separated by some terrible and tragic accident from all that had made it whole. As with most children who grow up in large families, I had a fascination with orphans and would often imagine what it would be like to be orphaned myself. Sometimes I would dream that a flood or a tornado would come and tear me away from my sprawling family, casting me out into the larger world like the main character in the TV show *Kung Fu*. What would I do if that happened? Where would I go? How would I survive? The prospect was terrifying, yet alluring, too.

One afternoon a wreck arrived at the salvage yard that seemed to encapsulate this notion of tragic and thrilling orphanhood perfectly. I vividly recall the moment the flatbed truck hauling the car pulled up before the Front, the way all of the parts men and mechanics and body men poured out as one to see it. The car on the flatbed was a bright orange Porsche 911—or rather half a Porsche 911.* The other half of the car

*My brother Alan claims the car was a Spyder 550. My father remembers it, vaguely, as a Triumph Spitfire. In my mind, however, the car will always be a Porsche 911.

had been chopped off (so Kenny the parts man claimed) when the "drunkass fool" who was driving it "flooded the engine on some railroad tracks north of Oklahoma City." Ordinarily, a car hit in the front and dragged for miles by a freight train would be worthless, but as my brother David quickly explained, Porsche 911s had their engines *in the rear*, and so, miraculously, this particular car was still worth quite a lot ("a mint," was how my brother put it), provided, of course, that a usable front end could be found for it.

For years after this, the wrecked Porsche sat under a tarp on the back lot of the salvage yard, a lonely import amid a sea of automobiles made in Detroit, while my father and everyone else who worked at the salvage yard listened to the radio for the words we so longed to hear: *Boys, listen up, we just come into some front end parts for a Porsche 911 . . .* Whenever I caught a glimpse of the orange car beneath its bright blue tarpaulin, my mind would begin to race, imagining all of the 911s out there in the world, each of them perfect in its own way, and yet at least one of them destined to be involved in some terrible accident, its front end cut away and shipped over vast distances to become one with *our* 911. When, in college, I was assigned to write a paper on the Thomas Hardy poem "The Convergence of the Twain," with its famous lines describing the building of the *Titanic* and the simultaneous growth of the iceberg that would sink it ("Alien they seemed to be; / No mortal eye could see / The intimate welding of their later history"), I could not help but think of the orange Porsche and the terrible desire and disappointment that engulfed it.

"When do you think we'll find it?" I would ask my father at least once a week.

"Find what?" he'd ask absently.

"The other half of the 911."

"Who knows?" he'd answer, shrugging. "It's an import. Parts for those don't come along every day of the week."

"Maybe someone else will get stalled on a railroad track," I speculated. "Only this time, he'll get almost the *whole* way across, and when the train comes, it will smack the car in the *rear,* not the front."

"Maybe," my father said. "I wouldn't hold my breath, though."

Stretching off a quarter of a mile behind the main buildings was the Yard proper with its row upon row of wrecked Buicks, Cadillacs, Chevys, Chryslers, Dodges, Fords, Oldsmobiles, Plymouths, Pontiacs, and so on, some of the cars stacked one atop the other like layers in a wedding cake, each of them guarded by roving bands of junkyard dogs, chiefly German shepherds and Doberman pinschers, with a few angry mutts thrown in for good measure. Often the hoods, trunks, and front or back doors of these cars stood open, creating a bizarre, stopped-in-time, Pompeii-like atmosphere. Everywhere was the evidence of Fate in the form of head-on collisions, rollovers, fire, and flood. The Yard itself was littered with more signs of the apocalypse, everything from shattered window glass to twisted sheet metal to headless dolls and solitary shoes and other debris that had come into the place along with the wrecks. In this sense, the Yard more than earned its traditional moniker of "automobile graveyard."

Looting this graveyard was my fondest occupation. Whenever a fresh wreck was dropped at the gate, I'd be the first to go through it, ransacking the glove compartment and truck for hidden treasure. I was rarely disappointed. On top of the usual horde of loose change, road maps, jumper cables, and tire tools, I found marbles, bats and baseballs, old paperbacks (Louis L'Amour was especially popular), secret stashes of *Hustler* and *Penthouse* magazines, costume jewelry of varying degrees of gaudiness, playing cards, pocket knives, Zippo lighters, sleeping bags, beach chairs, cigar boxes full of old photographs and diaries, fireworks, spent and unspent ammo. Unless it was deemed to be particularly valuable or dangerous, I was allowed to keep everything I found.

Some of the more mangled wrecks had bloodstains on the upholstery or even bits of human hair jutting from cracks in the windshield. At first, such sights gave me the creeps, but after a while they lost their power to scare me, and I treated them with the same air of professional detachment with which a forensic pathologist might view a fresh corpse. Only rarely did a new find make me feel the nearness of death. I remember one such instance with chilling clarity. For years, I had wanted a catcher's glove of a particular make and model (a Rawlings K3-H, let's call it), but since baseball was not one of my better sports and the rag-tag team I played on had an older glove I could use, I could never convince my parents to buy me one. Then one day I crawled into the back of a wrecked Corvair and there, wedged under the front passenger seat, was an almost brand new K3-H. Not believing my luck, I slipped the glove on my hand and held it out before me as though catching a pitch. It fit perfectly. Indeed, the mitt felt as if it had been made for my hand and no other. But then I noticed something that caused me to shake the glove off my hand as quickly as if I had felt a spider lurking in one of the finger holes. There, written in black permanent marker across the web of the glove, was the name ROBBY—*my* name, exactly as I spelled it. That the handwriting looked nothing like my own or my mother's did not abate my alarm. Somewhere out there in the world beyond the salvage yard, a second me, a ghastly twin or doppelganger, waited to do me harm—of this I was thoroughly convinced.

That whole outer realm of the salvage yard was ruled over by a strange and fascinating creature known to denizens of the salvage yard as "Yard Man." Unlike his more sophisticated cousins in the Front or the body shop, Yard Man worked outside the whole day through and in all kinds of weather—rain, sleet, snow, burning sun. To the parts guys, many of whom had finished high school and maybe even some college, Yard Man was a clumsy, unsophisticated brute. A vandal at heart, his stock-in-trade was force and speed, not precision. Ask a mechanic to pull a motor from a car, and he'd roll it into a bay in his shop and begin a careful disassembly process that included draining the radiator, unhooking the battery, loosening a dozen different clamps, belts, hoses, and mounts. Ask Yard Man to perform the same task, and he'd throw a chain around the motor, winch it up, and then cut everything holding the motor to the car with a blowtorch. Within minutes, the motor would lurch free and Yard Man would haul it, swinging on its chain like a pendulum, to the wash bay, where a grease-covered underling (often one of my teenaged brothers) would steam it off with a high-powered hose.

All day long, Yard Man roared up and down the narrow sand roads of the salvage yard atop a strange, homemade vehicle called a "goose." A goose was usually a retired army truck with the cab torn off, a roll cage welded into its place, and a crane-like winch mounted on the front. Other tools of Yard Man's trade—acetylene torch, sledgehammer, straight and angled crowbars—were mounted catch-as-catch-can along the sides and back. Whenever Yard Man took a coffee or bathroom break, I would climb into the high, still-warm seat of his abandoned goose and imagine myself rampaging through the world like a tank commander in a war movie. *Pow! Boom! Ka-Bam!* I would free all of the prisoners! Rain missiles on the enemy! Young women and girls would run alongside me in the rubble-strewn streets, blowing me kisses! Then, when Yard Man emerged from his break to reclaim his goose, I'd imagine that an enemy grenade had been lobbed into the tank and my only hope of survival was a daring leap to safety.

Five or six different Yard Men worked for my father during the years he owned the salvage yard, but the one I remember best was a baldheaded, pit bull–like man named Billy Dan. Billy Dan had a deep crease in the top of his forehead and an upper lip the size of a lemon, both of these abnormalities the result of an accident involving a truck bumper that swung back from the goose winch and caught Billy Dan full in the face. As far as I could tell, the man was mute. He communicated through grunts, high-pitched squeals, and terrible dark-eyed looks. Although I admired Billy Dan as a fellow man-of-action, I was also deeply terrified of him. All he had to do was look at me and I would run the other way as fast as my sneaker-clad feet would carry me. Part of this fear had to do with the fact that my older brothers used to tease me, saying, "Mom and Dad have finally decided what to do with you. They're going to give you to Billy Dan. At first he wanted to *buy* you, but Dad wouldn't hear of that . . ." Somehow I had got it into my head that Billy Dan was a veteran of the Vietnam War, and in my mind, Vietnam vets were addle-minded psychopaths never more than one "flashback" away from murdering everyone around them. Who was to say that Billy Dan hadn't been tortured beyond limits in some faraway rice paddy and lived now only to exact his revenge on the innocent?

Even watching him smoke or eat was a scary thing. He always seemed to have a cigar jutting out beneath his lemon lip, and when he struck a match to relight the cigar, an action he performed hundreds of times a day, all of the terrible contours of his face would be illuminated. His favorite meal, which he took daily in a little break room just off the wash bay, was pickled eggs and pigs' feet with a side of saltine crackers. The eggs he covered in salt and pepper before consuming them in a single bite. When these were gone he moved on to the pigs' feet, sucking the meat from bone and tendon before spitting the white knuckles onto the floor before him, a terrible sight to behold. Once, when I was sitting in the break room with him, Billy Dan attempted to share his lunch with me, his hand jutting out into the space between us to reveal a pig's foot resting atop a clean paper towel.

"No thanks," I said.

But this only caused him to shake the tidbit before me, his terrible green eyes urging me to try it.

"Okay," I said, afraid to give any other answer. But when I put the pig's foot in my mouth, and felt the cold, rubbery flesh on my tongue, I immediately gagged, spitting the unclean thing out at Billy Dan's feet.

He squealed with delight, holding his head back to reveal a single upper tooth, just to the right of his nose. Seeing that lonely tooth shook me even more than seeing the white pigs' knuckles arrayed on the floor.

As terrified as I was of Billy, his mere presence in the Yard often made me feel safer and less alone. One day, he even saved my life—or at least I believed he did. I was lying on my back beneath a junker Impala, pretending to change the oil, when suddenly I heard a rattling sound just to the left of my ear. Slowly I rolled my eyes in that direction, and coiled next to me, just inside the car's front tire, was a rattlesnake. I froze, my mouth going dry, heart beating wildly within my chest. I knew it was the end. Any second and the snake would bite me in the face or neck, and I'd be filled with poison and die. But then, just when I was about to give up the ghost, I heard the roar of Billy Dan's goose coming down the sand road at my feet. Eyes still closed, I focused on that sound as it grew louder and louder. Finally Billy Dan's goose shot past in a cloud of diesel smoke, and as the sound of it died away, I opened my eyes to see that the snake was gone, as vanished from this earth as if St. Patrick himself had appeared to banish it.

More terrifying than snakes and ogres were the junkyard dogs my father kept on the place to guard the parts from thieves. He always had a soft spot in his heart, a special love, for these terrible brutes, and they returned this love twentyfold. My father was the only person at the salvage yard who could go into their kennel near the racks of hubcaps to feed them, just as he was the only person who could fit their mouths with the leather muzzles they wore during the day so they wouldn't bite customers. Theirs was a jealous, protective love. Woe be unto the customer who argued with or raised his voice around my father, for he would soon find a growling, low-slung German shepherd poised next to him, as if awaiting the command to kill. My father never bought, bred, or went out of his way to acquire any of these dogs. People brought them to him. A station wagon or pickup would roll to a stop in front of the office, a harried-looking man would get out and ask for my father, and the two of them would stand talking and looking through the windows of the car at the beast jailed within.

"He's been biting people," the man would begin. "I promised the neighbors I'd have him put down. But then a guy told me you sometimes take on dogs like this."

"Does he bite *you?*" my father would ask.

And the man would answer with a yes or no, and the dog would be brought out of the car on a chain or leash, and my father would look it over, and if the vibe was good and he liked the dog, soon he would be scratching behind its ears and talking to it in a low voice. "Been biting people, huh, Shep? That's no good. No good at all . . ."

A little longer and the dog would be licking his hand or burying its head in his lap.

"What do you think?" the man would ask.

"I can't promise you I'll keep him," my father would say with a shrug. "But we can certainly give him a try."

In this way, my father acquired a half dozen or more junkyard dogs, all of them troubled in some way, unmanageable by anyone but him. Almost without exception, they were "one person" dogs, saving all of their affection and trust for my father. Everyone else—including women, children, the elderly and infirm—they looked upon with distrust and hatred.

I first came into contact with these dogs when I was four or five years old, and from the beginning I was deeply afraid of them. Although my father kept the dogs muzzled during the day, that didn't stop them from chasing me and knocking me down. I'd be playing in some remote part of the Yard, and out of nowhere the dogs would appear, their presence announced by a low growl from somewhere deep inside their throats. Once, I was playing twenty yards or so from their kennel when two of the dogs cornered me. I stood up, terrified, careful not to look the dogs in the eye. *I'm done for,* I thought. *They're gonna kill me for sure.*

But then my father appeared and called the dogs off. "What were you doing to annoy them?" he asked.

"Nothing," I said.

"Well, I wouldn't let them see you playing with those," he said, nodding at the hubcaps scattered across the concrete floor. "They eat their dinner in those. They probably thought you were going to steal their food."

Although I was happy to be rescued, I still held a special grudge against the dogs—and, in a way, against my father—that did not abate until the day I happened to see them in action.

It was a Sunday morning. We had been at Mass in town and still wore our church clothes when my father and I drove out to the salvage yard to give the dogs their breakfast. My father unlocked the door to the Front and switched on lights one by one as we walked down the long corridor past the hubcaps to the closet where the dog food was kept. Having filled a couple of hubcaps with kibble, we carried them outside to the wash bay, where my father whistled for the dogs to come get their breakfast. Usually when he did this, the dogs came bounding from two or three different parts of the Yard at once. On that day, however, none of the dogs came. All we got was a bark or two from some distant part of the Yard.

"Where are they?" I asked.

"I don't know," my father said. "You stay here and I'll go and see."

"No," I answered, afraid. "I'm not staying here. What if they come back?"

He thought about this a moment, then said, "All right, you can come. But stay right by me, and if I tell you to stay back, you stay back. Got it?"

"Yes." I took his hand in mine and held it tight. We began to zigzag across the Yard in the direction from which we had heard the barks.

The ground rose slightly in that direction, and wrecked cars were stacked high on either side of us. As a result, we couldn't see more than a dozen yards ahead of us at any time. However, the closer we got, the louder the dogs barked. Finally we turned a corner, and there, high atop a wrecked van, sat a couple of long-haired men in dirty jeans and ripped T-shirts. Beneath them on all sides of the van were five or six drooling, howling yard dogs.

"What's going on?" my father asked the men in an even voice.

"Not much," one of the men offered sheepishly.

"Where did you come in?"

"Around back," the other man said, pointing his chin in that direction.

"Did you cut the fence?"

"No. Climbed over."

"What happened to your arm?" my father asked. Only then did I notice that one of the men was holding his arm a little funny, as if he had injured it.

"Dog bit it."

"I see," my father said, nodding his head. "Tell me this. If I let you boys down, are you coming over that fence again?"

"No, boss," the first man said. "You can count on that."

After the men were gone back over the fence and the dogs were greedily choking down their kibble, I asked my father who these men were, expecting him to answer with some generic term like "burglars" or "parts thieves." Instead, he shrugged and rattled off their first and last names. "They're brothers," he added. "Their father and uncles used to come over that same fence twenty years ago. It's kind of a family tradition, I guess you'd say."

I didn't know what to say to that. In my mind, he should have had the men thrown into jail. What was the point of catching them if you were only going to let them go? As for the dogs, although I had gained a newfound respect for the work they did at the salvage yard, I still didn't trust or like them. I just knew

that if they ever caught me in the Yard when my father wasn't
around, they'd tear me to pieces with the same jealous ferocity
they used on thieves.

Of the dozen or so men who worked at the salvage yard
at any one time, among them Yard Men, body men, engine spe-
cialists, and front office help, one of the most fascinating was a
half-crippled mechanic named Speck. Of course, Speck wasn't
his real name, but it was the name sewn on the pocket of his
light blue mechanic's uniform. Speck talked with a slight lisp
and walked with a limp, the result of a motorcycle accident
that should have earned him a handsome settlement, had he
not been cheated out of it by insurance company lawyers—so
he claimed, at any rate, heaping terrible insults upon the heads
of lawyers everywhere. In addition to his uniform, he wore ugly
boots with thick, oil-resistant soles. His glasses were black and
held together in the middle with electrical tape, the lenses thick
and pitted with debris from the grinder and sandblaster.

Speck was an opinionated slanderer of everyone of a different race, color, or creed than himself, as well as anyone deemed
by him to be "stupid." His natural mode of discourse was the
incoherent rant, the terribleness of which was compounded by
his lisp and the fact that his mouth was always full of Redman
chewing tobacco. To most people, all of this would have made
Speck insufferable, but I thought he was the most interesting
person I had ever met. Unlike everyone else in my life, Speck
showed no sign of even realizing I was a child. He cussed freely
before me, belched and farted, made dubious pronouncements
about the world and the people in it. Taking out his tobacco for
a chew, he would ask if I wanted some. When I said I didn't, he
just shrugged, as if to say, "Your loss."

Speck's specialty as a mechanic was the "stretching" of
trucks. My father and Uncle Harold would fly down to the
used truck auction in Oklahoma City and bring back ten or
twelve Cain's Coffee trucks. One by one, Speck would cut the

trucks in half and lengthen their frames by seven or eight feet, so they could be fitted with hoists and resold as wheat trucks. Hanging out in Speck's shop one summer, I came to know the stretching process inside out, and before long I was elevated to the status of gofer, running after whatever tool Speck might need at the time.

"Get me that hammer and punch," Speck might say over his shoulder. When I brought them to him, he would snort his thanks and offer up some tidbit of Speck wisdom. "You know, don't you, that you and your whole tribe are gonna roast in the fires of hell?"

"What tribe is that, Speck?" I'd ask, thrilled by such talk.

"Papists."

"But I'm not a part of that tribe, Speck—or any, that I know of."

"Sure you are. You're Catholic, ain't you?"

"Yes."

"Baptized as a baby?"

"I guess so."

"Well, there you go. You weren't *immersed*. But that's only the beginning of why you're going to hell . . ."

And off he'd go on some new angle I thrilled to hear. I didn't always understand, much less believe, the things Speck talked about. It was the free-flowing nature of his discourse I loved, the way he could just *turn it on* the way you might turn on a spigot, and here everything came spilling out in a gush. In another life, he might have been a shock jock, or maybe a radio preacher. I'm sure he could have thrilled a certain kind of audience with his impromptu rants.

Then one day, toward the end of the summer I spent hanging around his shop, something happened that caused me to revise my estimation of Speck. We had just installed a new radiator in one of the Cain's trucks and were hunting around the shop for the red five-gallon can Speck kept water in. "Where the hell is it?" he raved. "The sumbitches! Don't those Yard Men know to keep their filthy hands off my stuff?"

When we finally located the can, on a slab of greasy cement where the Yard Men parked their gooses, it was only to discover that someone had used it as a catch can for an oil change. "Fools! Idiots! I'll kill them all—the worthless sumbitches!" Speck yelled, emptying the can into a sticker patch before limping angrily back into his shop.

It took ten minutes of scrubbing with soap and water to get the can back to its original condition. That done, we dried the top and sides with a shop rag, and Speck took some yellow paint we used to label parts and began to carefully mark the can in big block letters. *W O T* . . . Here he paused a moment, glancing over his shoulder at me as if he had just realized I was there. Then, shaking his head and muttering something under his breath, he finished by carefully painting the letter *R* followed by an exclamation mark.

I stood there, paralyzed by confusion. Why had Speck written *W O T R !* when he clearly meant *W A T E R !?* Was this some kind of industry-wide alternative spelling? If so, why adopt it, when the result was a savings of only one letter? Then it hit me. *He can't spell.*

Some part of the change sweeping over me must have communicated itself to Speck, because when I looked up, he was frowning at me.

"What?" he asked.

"Nothing," I said, unwilling to share my discovery with the man most affected by it.

Not long after, I switched my admiration to another salvage yard personality—Challo, the body man. While the other men who worked for my father all wore the same uniform of dark blue trousers along with a light blue shirt with a name tag—"Larry," "Bill"—and an oval patch bearing the words "B & B Auto Parts" on each pocket (indeed, my father himself wore this uniform religiously), Challo could not be bothered. At best, he regarded the dress code as optional. If he wore the pants, it would be with an old football jersey or a black Harley-Davidson T-shirt. On days when he deigned to wear the uniform shirt, it would be with jeans or shorts, the shirt unbuttoned, its tail flopping behind him. Challo was a dark man with nearly black eyes and long black hair he covered with a bandana or a polka-dot beanie of the kind favored by welders. When he bothered to shave, he went in for long sideburns and a Fu Manchu mustache. Indeed, he claimed to have created the style himself. "Broadway Joe ain't got nothing on me," he would declare, smiling to show a gold cap on one of his front teeth.

It was this style of Challo's that appealed so strongly to me—that and his sense of freedom. I remember asking my father how it was that Challo seemed to operate under a different code and different rules than the other men who worked for him at the salvage yard. He just shrugged the matter off the way a philosopher might shrug off a famous conundrum. "He's a body man," he explained. "They're just a different breed, that's all."

When I asked what that meant, he went on to explain that an experienced body man was more like an independent contractor than a regular employee. "They're like hairdressers," he said, offering a comparison that stunned me to my core. "When they get tired of working in one shop, or don't like the rules there, or have a falling-out with the boss, they just move down the street to the next shop, and then the next. Most of the body men in this town have worked at pretty much every shop in town, some of them more than once."

When I pressed further, amazed that he would rehire someone who had quit on him months or years before, he made an even more startling comparison. "Body work isn't something just *anybody* can do," he said. "It takes a certain touch. An artist's touch."

Once the comparison had been made, I could see that it was so. The body shop itself, with its floodlights and pervasive odor of paint and bizarre tools for pounding dents out of sheet metal, was like nothing so much as an artist's studio. An air of bohemian cool pervaded the place, surrounding all of the men who worked there. The act of smoothing out body putty or laying down a coat of lacquer with the paint gun required poise and precision. There was nothing of the grease monkey in it, no gasoline fumes or black dirt beneath the fingernails. The job was not to repair so much as to transform.

When I say Challo was an artist, I mean he was a man of ideas with the means to make those ideas a reality. Once he sent me to get him a cheeseburger and fries from his favorite burger joint down the road from the salvage yard. Because the place was more than a mile away, and I had to walk there and back, by the time I returned the food was lukewarm.

"What took you so long?" Challo asked, pulling a soggy fry from the bag and inspecting it with a grimace. "This shit is cold, man."

"It's a long walk," I said.

"Well, take your bike next time."

"I don't have one," I lied.

"Really?" Challo asked, raising his black eyebrows in a way that showed he was already entertaining some outlandish new idea.

Not long after this, he showed up at the salvage yard with an old Schwinn with rusted fenders and rims and an ugly faux leopard-skin banana seat. The bike looked suspiciously as if it had been lifted from a school playground or someone's back-yard, but I didn't ask about that. For the next couple of days, while other projects he should have been working on sat wait-ing, Challo lavished his full attention on the Schwinn. First he stripped the bike down to its frame and sanded off all of the old yellow paint. Then he hung the frame on a wire and hit it with a coat of brown primer and two or three coats of candy apple red. The next morning, after the paint had dried, he replaced the bike's original handlebars with a pair of chrome bars he took off a wrecked motorcycle. Then he cut the bike's chrome sissy bar down so that the back of the banana seat rested, fender-like, an inch above the back tire. The seat itself he covered in some black leather upholstery cut out of the backseat of a wrecked Cadil-lac. By now, other guys at the salvage yard had taken an interest in the project as well, and they brought in new tires, wheels, and pedals. Finished, the red Schwinn gleamed in the sun like some extravagantly restored vehicle in a classic car show.

"Well, what do you think?" Challo asked.

"It's great," I said, fumbling for a way to express my gratitude.

"Shit, man, that bike ain't *great*," he returned. "That bike is *bad-ass*, you know what I'm saying? BAD-ASS!"

"Bad-ass," I repeated.

"Now you're talking."

Reaching into his paint-splattered Levis, the body man pulled out a five-dollar bill and waved it in front of his nose. "Cheeseburger with extra mustard and onions, man. And this time, that shit better not be *cold*."

The idea of the artist as renegade and rebel, as someone who marched to the beat of his own drum, a professional in every sense but bound to no man, answerable only to his art and his own internal agenda—the salvage yard was where that intoxicating idea first blossomed into life for me.

O

I was at school the morning Kenny and the other parts men finally located the other half of the wrecked Porsche 911 that had sat for such a long time beneath a tarp at the back of the salvage yard. Throughout the week or so it took for the car to be picked up in Georgia or California and hauled all the way back to Dodge City, I remained in a state of suspended animation, imagining over and over again the semimagical process by which the two cars would be fused into one. In my mind, the two wrecks were mirror images of one another—both the same color of orange with the same chocolate brown interior, the only real difference being the fact that one had been hit in the front, the other in the rear. My mother dropped me at the salvage yard after basketball practice the day the car arrived, and I ran through the Front and past the long corridor to a spot outside of Speck's shop where both cars had been dragged. Sitting there next to the orange Porsche was not the clone I had imagined but rather a powder blue 911 that looked as if it had been put through the car crusher. I had never seen a car so destroyed. It had no windows or wheels, and the car's roof was so crushed that it rested on the tops of the ruined bucket seats. I had heard from my father that the car had been "rolled," but I didn't expect it to look like this— as though someone had driven it off a cliff.

"Man, that car isn't *anything* like the other one," I said. "It's *destroyed*."

"Nah, man," Challo said, smiling. "We'll fix it up nice. You'll see."

I remained doubtful. As much time as I had spent around the salvage yard, as many project cars as I'd seen the guys take on, including two different late-model stock cars my brother Alan raced on a local dirt track, I had never witnessed a project this daunting. A Porsche 911 was in a different league entirely than the Cain's Coffee trucks and run-of-the-mill Chevys and Fords the guys at the salvage yard were used to working on. And didn't Speck live in a house one of my brothers described as a "cracker box"? Hadn't Challo gone on a bender so huge that money had to be wired to El Paso, Texas, just so he could catch a Greyhound back to Dodge City?

So it was with skepticism that I looked on as the powder blue 911 was dragged into Speck's shop and stripped down to its frame, which he and my brother Alan went to work straightening. When that was done, and more time was found, the wheels and engine from the orange 911 were mounted on the frame, and body parts from both cars were brought to Challo for reconditioning. Here I thought the whole process would speed up, but once again I was wrong. "You can't rush a job like this," Challo declared, as slowly, over five or six weeks, he worked his way through each of the body components, straightening it, pounding the dents out, laying down thin layers of body putty, and then sanding these down until they were smooth and ready to receive a coat of gray primer. Only when all of this work was done, and the body parts began to be fitted onto the straightened frame of the car, did I begin to see the possibilities. By then there was no blue 911 or orange 911. In their place was an entirely new car, one that had not existed before and that did not belong, so far as I could tell, to anyone—not my father or the parts men or Speck and Challo or, least of all, me. "This motherfucker's gonna *fly*, just you watch," Challo would say, winking. And yet, still I would not let myself believe—not entirely.

Finally, after six months of work done piecemeal, as time allowed, the 911 was finished enough that it could be taken out for a test drive. By then, the mechanics had gone over the engine with a fine-toothed comb, and the thing purred like the exotic and powerful beast it was. By ones and twos, all of the guys who worked at the salvage yard got a chance to take the car on a run down Minneola Road, a long ribbon of asphalt stretching off into the horizon in the direction of Oklahoma. Each time the car roared off on yet another maiden voyage, I would stand in the gravel lot before the Front, listening as the sound of the engine faded off into the distance. In the silence that followed, my heart would sink and sink, and I would begin to believe that both the car and the man driving it were gone forever, and I would never see either one again. But then my turn came. My brother Tom, who was maybe seventeen at the time, was tossed the keys. He turned to me as he climbed behind the wheel, and said, "Get in, fool. It's time to roll."

I climbed into the passenger's seat, and we took off down Minneola Road, my brother shifting up through the ladder of gears with a strange smile animating his face. At eighty-five or ninety, he turned and yelled into the wind, "Third gear! I'm in fucking third gear!" Hearing this, I laid my head back against the seat the way the characters on *Star Trek* did when the *Enterprise* was about to enter warp speed. Challo was right. The motherfucker did fly, no question about it.

Not a week after this, I showed up at the salvage yard early on a Saturday morning and straightaway went looking for the 911, which I had heard had been painted the same shade of candy apple red as my bike. However, when I got to the spot in Challo's shop where the car had sat awaiting its final coat of paint not two days before, I found that the car was gone. Not finding Challo there either, I ran into Speck's shop next door and asked breathlessly, "Where's Challo? Where's the 911?"

"Challo?" Speck said. "You think Challo comes in this early? He's probably still in bed, sleeping one off."

"And the 911?"

"Your dad sold it," Speck said, shrugging. "Guy flew in from Atlanta last night to pick it up."

I stood there, shaking my head and remembering what Kenny the parts man had told me the time I had cried about his selling my favorite hubcap. *Well, what did you think we did around here? Play with ourselves?* I still didn't get it.

A couple of years after this, my father and uncle sold the salvage yard, and my father used the money to buy a farm, where I would later be put to work much as my older brothers had been at B & B. It was the end of one era and the beginning of another. Unable to imagine my father without his blue uniform, I asked my mother what he would wear to work now that he was giving up the salvage business.

"Oh, he'll wear khaki pants or jeans, maybe a nice plaid shirt," she replied.

I couldn't picture it. To me, my father would always wear the dark blue pants and light blue shirt with the red-outlined breast patches reading "Bill" and "B & B Auto." The future, full of yearnings and mistakes and the responsibilities of manhood, loomed like some yawning void, filled with uncertainty.

The Identity Factory

"Never forget *who* and, more importantly, *what* you are," Monsignor Husman said, shaking a white finger at us where we sat in the front pews of the old mission-style church a mile east of Dodge City's infamous Boot Hill. "Just because you're going over to the junior high next year doesn't mean you can ignore everything you've been taught and start acting like a bunch of little fools. You're one of *us*. You *represent* us. Is that understood?"

"Yes, Monsignor," we intoned as one.

It was the spring of 1979, a few weeks before graduation at Sacred Heart Cathedral School, and the entire eighth grade, about fifty of us, had been pulled from class and ushered into the empty cathedral to hear Monsignor's parting words of advice. Because there was no Catholic secondary school in Dodge City, starting in ninth grade, we would be obliged to attend the public junior high, a den of licentiousness about which we'd heard much over the years and which most of us could not wait to experience for ourselves. We were Catholic school kids, heirs to a long and mostly proud tradition that included strict codes of conduct and dress, daily Mass and religion class, out-of-date textbooks held together with Elmer's glue and duct tape, the monthly gauntlet of confession, the constant pressure to try hard and succeed at all things, nuns as teachers, priests as terrible figures of judgment, the early inculcation of responsibility and guilt, and, above all, the insistence, repeated ad infinitum, that we were nothing at all like our peers in public school—that godless horde who went about their heathenish ways completely unaware of the fact that the ground on which our town was built had been consecrated by a Catholic priest (Father Juan Padilla) three hundred years before the first settlers arrived.

"If we've done right by you," Monsignor concluded his speech, "then the lessons you've learned here ought to stay with you not just through junior high and high school but *for the rest of your lives.*"

Here I rolled my eyes just a bit. For while there was little in Monsignor's speech I disagreed with, I was also a newly minted teenager and could not wait to be free from that place that had been both a refuge and a prison to me for almost as long as I could remember.

In ways I still struggle to understand, I owe my existence to the Catholic Church, or at least to an order of energetic nuns called the Sisters of St. Joseph. It was the Sisters who raised my father for the first three months of his life, stowing him away in their convent near St. Anthony's Hospital after the woman who gave birth to him in October 1933 returned to her home in eastern Kansas. It was the Sisters—one of them, at any rate, Sister Adeline, who worked in the laundry at St. Anthony's—who eventually found a permanent home for him among her relatives in the diocese, the transfer taking place under the bishop's watchful eye in January 1934. It was these same Sisters who educated my father, given the middle name of Joseph in honor of their patron saint, when he began school at Sacred Heart in the fall of 1939. Finally, it was the Sisters who converted my mother, a young nursing student at St. Mary of the Plains College, thus setting the stage for my parents' Catholic wedding in 1952 and ensuring that the family they started soon after continued to grow past the point where more sensible people would have called it quits.

Given this history, there was never any question about what school I would attend or who my teachers would be. I was a Rebein, after all, and Rebeins everywhere traced their heritage to the same little town in the Soest district of Germany at the center of which a statue of the Virgin Mary had stood for over three hundred years. On my first day at Sacred Heart, my mother escorted me as far as the door to one of the basement classrooms, where we were met by a tall, imposing woman with thick, Buddy Holly–style glasses. A modern nun, Sister Anthony Marie did not go in for the traditional habit with its formfitting coif and flowing tunic. Instead she wore knee-length polyester skirt-and-blouse combos, with a small gold cross adorning her ample chest, and a veil the size of a folded napkin pinned to the back of her bouffant hair. Bending at the waist to greet me that first day, she took my chin between her forefinger and thumb and said in a loud, laughing voice, "Young man, you've got some *awfully* big shoes to fill."

As Sister said this, she and my mother exchanged knowing winks, and I understood all at once that the two of them were in cahoots, and if a dispute ever arose between Sister and me, I could not expect my mother to protect me or even to take my side. I had been farmed out. From that point on, I would have to fend for myself.

"Be good for Sister!" Mom called as she disappeared down that long, narrow hallway.

"I'll try," I answered.

To be good in Sister Anthony Marie's class was to *be still*, a double imperative meaning both to hush and to sit still. But I was by nature a fidgety, hyperactive child, constantly talking out of turn and grabbing things that weren't mine. I can still vividly recall Sister's voice booming down on me from the front of the classroom. *Mr. Rebein, sit down! Mr. Rebein, you're talking again! Mr. Rebein, keep your hands to yourself!* I wanted to obey; I pinched myself and whispered in a low voice, so no one else would hear, *Be good! Try to remember!* But I would forget again soon enough, and the cycle would begin again.

To make matters worse, I started first grade with a cast on my right arm, the result of trying to walk the "tightrope" of a neighbor's clothesline. This made writing, the principal activity in Sister Anthony Marie's class, nearly impossible for me. I sat there with a No. 2 pencil gripped awkwardly in my left hand, my eyes glued to the long hand of the clock as it made its slow march toward recess. "Is it time yet?" I'd blurt out every few minutes. "Can we go outside? How long until we go?"

"*I'll* tell you when it's time," Sister would reply. "Now will you please sit down and try to be quiet?"

"Yes, Sister," I'd answer.

Then one day, as was inevitable, Sister's frustrations and my own collided in a single, cathartic moment of violence. We were standing in line, waiting for the hallway outside our classroom to empty of other children so we could go out to recess. I watched Sister closely, waiting for her to raise the yardstick she used to guard the door and keep us in line. But the signal didn't come and didn't come. Finally, I heard the other first-grade teacher, Mrs. Wagner, call from the end of the hallway that all was clear, and I bolted from my place in line and made for the door. Seeing me coming, Sister crouched low and called for me to stop, but by then, it was already too late; both our fates were sealed. As I tried to get past her, Sister grabbed me by my left arm, spun me around, and in a single, practiced movement, whacked me hard across my right arm with the dreaded yardstick.

"Ouch! You hit me!" I howled, more out of fright than pain, for in fact my cast had absorbed the entire blow.

"That's right," Sister said, breathing hard but otherwise calm. "And I'll do it again, too, if you don't behave."

I stood there, tears running down my cheeks. Apart from some mistreatment at the hands of my brothers—thumped knuckles, Indian burns, and the like—no one had so much as laid a hand on me before. Witnessing my shock, Sister sent the rest of the class out to recess with Mrs. Wagner, then sat down next to me in a chair several sizes too small for her.

"Oh, it's not so bad," she said, wiping at my tears with a tissue she kept folded beneath the wristband of her Timex. Hearing this, I stole a glance at Sister's face, expecting to encounter a look of anger there. Instead she just tossed her head back and laughed. "You look *just* like your father," she said. "Did you know that?"

"My father has black hair," I countered, not trusting the change in her. "Mine is brown."

"That's true," Sister said. "But you're his spitting image all the same."

And with this, Sister reached out with the same hand she had used to hit me and began to knead the tension out of my back and shoulders. At the time, I knew nothing about the circumstances of my father's birth and subsequent adoption. Nor could I look into the future and see that this would be the one and only time that a teacher at Sacred Heart would hit me. All I knew was that something intimate and profound had just passed between Sister and me, and we understood each other now in a way that even my mother and I did not. We were forever bound together, like Jesus and his cross; she was my burden, and I was hers.

"Can I go outside now?" I asked, after another minute had passed.

"Of course you can," Sister said.

And so I did, bolting from that room as though shot from a cannon.

Later that year, we began our preparations for First Communion. Having seen my older brothers go through this ritual, I thought I knew what to expect: new clothes, a sizable haul of presents, a white frosted cake in the shape of a lamb, and so on. But these were but the trappings of the sacrament, Sister Anthony Marie informed us. The reality was something deeper. "Unless you eat the flesh of the son of man and drink his blood," she quoted to us from the Gospel of John, "you do not have life within you."

What to make of that? I wondered. I mean, surely the statement couldn't be, you know, *literally* true . . . could it? I raised my hand and put the question to Sister.

"The statement means exactly what it says," she answered.

A hush fell over the room. Then a kid in the back announced in a loud whisper, "I'm not drinking any blood. What do they think we are, *vampires*?"

My classmates laughed raucously at this joke, but I was haunted by the image it brought to mind. At Mass each morning, I watched with horror as the kids from the upper grades filed up to Monsignor and stuck out their tongues to receive the host. *What did it taste like?* I wondered. *Actual flesh and blood? Two-thousand-year-old flesh and blood? What would I do when the smell of it hit me? Puke? Pass out? Turn tail and run?* I carried these fears like a tumor, confessing them to no one—not to Sister, my parents, even my classmates or older brothers. I was too ashamed, too worried that I'd be laughed at or, worse, that all of my deepest fears would be confirmed.

Finally the big day arrived. I remember the heaviness and dread with which I slipped on my polished white shoes and clip-on tie. I felt as though I were being led off to my own execution. When the call to communion arrived, I rose along with my classmates and filed into the center aisle of the cathedral. The place was packed to the gills with classmates, relatives, and neighbors. Camera bulbs exploded in our faces, and Super 8's whirred loudly, their extension cords snaking off to connect with hidden outlets.

Soon enough, I made it to the front of the church, where Monsignor Temant, wearing a white robe with a huge red cross emblazoned on its front, raised the host before me.

"The body of Christ," he said in his loud voice.

I stood there, my jaw locked tight.

"The body of Christ," Monsignor repeated.

This is it, I thought. *I'm gonna throw up for sure.*

But as afraid as I was of what was about to happen, I was even more afraid of standing apart from my family and friends. *If this is what I am*, I thought, *then so be it*. Swallowing hard, I stuck out my tongue and hoped for the best. A young priest named Father Maize held a gold plate beneath my chin to catch the host should it fall, and a moment later, Monsignor deposited it on the tip of my outstretched tongue. I trapped the thing against the roof of my mouth and, careful to breathe through my nose only, began the long trek back to my pew. Halfway there, amid a crescendo of exploding camera lights, a stark realization began to steal over me. The host tasted like . . . a host, a dry piece of unleavened bread. Nothing more, nothing less.

"Do you feel any different?" people began to ask me as soon as Mass was over.

"No," I told them. "I don't feel any different. I feel just the same."

But the truth was, a great weight had been lifted from my shoulders. I had been cured, forever, of literalism. From that day forward, I would never believe in anything in quite the same way again.

O Sacred Heart was an institution that prided itself on hard work and academic achievement. A grade of C, which is to say anything below 86 percent, was thought to be a disaster and a disgrace, and any child who received such a grade soon heard about it from teachers, from parents, and especially from Monsignor Husman, who made it a point to visit each and every classroom to personally hand out quarterly report cards. Monsignor was not the sort to dwell on successes, preferring to highlight those areas where a student was struggling, or "scraping his nose," as Monsignor liked to put it.

"Let's see what we have here," he would say, adjusting a thick pair of bifocals on his bulbous nose. "B in religion. Well, that could be better, couldn't it? And what do we have here? B– in math! You're *scraping your nose,* young man, *scraping your nose!*" And so it would go. If there were any C's on the card—as there often were with mine—he would raise the volume and the theatrics, jerking the glasses from his face, the better to stare one down with his beady eyes. "Tell me," he would say. "Just what kind of nonsense have you been up to?"

As no good answer to that question existed, I soon learned to skip it altogether and go straight into my apology. "I'm sorry, Monsignor. I'll do better next time. I promise."

"Well, I should hope so!" the old priest would say, shaking his white head in bewilderment. "This entire report is completely unacceptable!"

Starting in fifth grade, the stakes rose even higher. Instead of having one teacher to answer to and please, suddenly we had three or four—each with a different agenda and a different set of expectations. Homework increased exponentially, becoming not just a chore but a full-blown ordeal involving an hour or more of concentrated effort each and every night.

At eleven years old, I didn't feel much like working. As soon as I got home from school, I would drop my books on the kitchen floor and head right back out the door, disappearing on my bike or skateboard and not returning until it was time for dinner. If my mother happened to ask me if I had done my homework, I would lie or promise to do it later. "I'll do it!" I'd whine. "Gosh! Get off my back!" But of course I didn't do it, rarely thinking of it again until the next morning, when it was already too late.

One teacher in particular caused me no end of distress. Her name was Sister Antonella, and she was known throughout the school for her unorthodox personality (she played twelve-string guitar and was obsessed with the "musical genius" of John Denver) and the often outrageous demands she made on students (quizzing us two or three times a week and assigning long lists of words and phrases to be committed to memory). A volatile person with expressive brown eyes and widely spaced teeth, Sister could be quite scary when she got into one of her rages. But she could also be surprisingly kind, as when she defended me after I was caught in a lie by another teacher, laughing the matter off by saying, "The boy's got a healthy imagination, that's all."

Unfortunately for me, however, Sister's primary subjects, English and spelling, were two of my very worst. The problem was not that I lacked aptitude—I later earned a PhD in English—but rather that I did not care to put in the time memorizing the long lists of words and phrases Sister was forever sending home with us. In one particularly torturous assignment, we were asked to memorize and recite before the class a list of forty-nine commonly used prepositions—*about, above, across, after, against, along, among, around, at, before, behind, below, beneath, beside, between, by, down, during, except, for, from, in, in front of, inside, instead of, into, like, near, of, off, on, on top of, onto, out of, outside, over, past, since, through, to, toward, under, underneath, until, up, upon, with, within, without . . .*

This list of words was the cause of both my downfall and my eventual resurrection in Sister's eyes. She had been after me for weeks to recite the words for a grade. The quarter was coming to an end, and she needed my score to complete her grade book. However, I put her off from one day to the next. I just needed another evening to practice, I would say, and then I would be ready. Finally, however, I had to admit the truth, which was that I hadn't even remembered to take the words home.

"That's your excuse?" Sister asked, looking at me with those terrible brown eyes of hers.

"Yes, Sister," I said, secretly glad that the crisis had come.

But then the day for first quarter report cards rolled around, and Monsignor, dressed as usual in a full-length black cassock with red buttons, called me to the front of the class so that he could read my grades aloud. A part of me still held out hope for a C in English, maybe even a B–. However, no sooner did Monsignor open my card than the blood seemed to drain from his face all at once, and I understood that the moment of my reckoning had arrived.

"*D– in English?*" the old priest bellowed. "*D in spelling? What on earth!*"

I was beyond scraping my nose now. I turned to look at Sister Antonella where she stood with her arms folded across her chest, staring me down in that steely way she had, chin and eyebrows slightly raised, as if to say, "Young man, even if the great John Denver himself were to plead your case in song, still I would be required to teach you this lesson."

That night, after the ordeal of getting my parents to sign the report, I went straight to my room and cleaned off the desk that up to this point had been used to display sports trophies and a collection of rocks I'd dug out of a drainage ditch that ran through my neighborhood. I remember the moment very clearly: the slow, sad resignation of it, the tedious business of getting out paper and pen, and the laboriousness of scratching out the words. *About, above, across, after . . .* I hated every second of it, but I understood, too, that a line of sorts had been crossed, and there could be no going back—then or ever.

By the end of the year, I had brought my pair of D's up to a B and a B–, respectively. That was no great shakes, of course, but it meant something to me—and, as it turned out, to Sister Antonella, too. On the last day of school, as I prepared to leave her class forever, Sister presented me with a hand-lettered card that read *Certificate for Continued Effort in English and Spelling.* On the outside of the card was a portrait of a rugged, Charlton Heston–like Jesus, while on the inside was a quotation from the New Testament: *I can do all things through Christ which strengtheneth me.*

I took some razzing from my older brothers on account of that card, but I didn't care. In defiance of them, I took the gaudy thing home and pinned it to the bulletin board above my desk, where it remained even after I had graduated from Sacred Heart and moved on to the public junior high across town.

Religion and academics aside, the single most important arena of endeavor at Sacred Heart was sports. Whether it was football or volleyball, basketball or wrestling, boys' sports or girls', the twin objectives were always the same—to play hard and win. To be found lacking in either of these areas was cause for considerable shame, and to fail at both of them at the same time was tantamount to having committed an actual sin. For this reason, teams from Sacred Heart rarely lost.

This point is illustrated by an incident involving my brother Joe. In the semifinals of the diocesan basketball tournament, which was held every year in Sacred Heart's gym, he and his fellow eighth graders played a lazy first half against a smaller school, falling behind by several baskets. Their coach, an intense man from New York named Bob Chilton, gave the team a good chewing out at halftime, then left them to stew in his words. All things considered, they had gotten off pretty easy, Joe thought. But then they heard what sounded like a metal trash can being kicked down the flight of stairs just outside the locker room door. A moment later, the door swung open, and Monsignor Temant stepped through, his face red and beaded with sweat. "I'd never seen him so mad before," Joe would say, remembering the event. "He kicked us out of our own locker room, told us to get our asses upstairs and run suicides until halftime was over. We won the game, of course. But even so, afterward we ran more suicides. Monsignor wanted to make sure we got the point. We got it, all right."

It was the same with every sport and at every level of competition, from fourth-grade wrestling to eighth-grade football. The object was not just to win but to send a message. If the opponent was another Catholic school, the message was that in the race to represent Christ and His Church, Sacred Heart was not about to be outworked or outplayed by anyone, let alone a puny parish from some backwater of the diocese. If, in contrast, the opponent was a larger public school, particularly one from Dodge City, then the message was that despite our mismatched uniforms and underdog status, teams from Sacred Heart were not in the habit of rolling over for anyone, especially not for a team of rich Protestants from a permissive school system that had long ago lost touch with values such as hard work, humility, and determination.

Our coaches in these holy wars were drawn from the ranks of former scholarship athletes at St. Mary of the Plains College, and a bizarrely high percentage of them hailed not from the plains of Kansas but from New York City. A recruiting pipeline of sorts had been established years before between some Catholic schools in New York and St. Mary's, and some of the players thus brought to Kansas stuck around for years after graduation, teaching in the upper grades at Sacred Heart and coaching the football and basket-ball teams. As a group, the New Yorkers were brash, loud, cocky, and hypercompetitive. They had grown up in tough, working-class parishes in Brooklyn or Queens, and they let us know on a regular basis that none of the challenges we encountered as religious minorities in a small town on the plains could compare to what they had faced on what they always called "the mean streets of New Yawk." Needless to say, we idolized these men and would have walked through fire to please them. To us, they represented the world beyond Sacred Heart and Dodge City—indeed, beyond Kansas itself—and we saw having them as teachers and coaches as a stroke of almost unbelievable good luck.

Like us, the New Yorkers viewed the games we played against our public school rivals as the biggest competitions of the year. And the biggest of these wasn't even an actual game but rather the annual scrimmage we played against the junior high's eighth-grade football team. The date of the scrimmage was known to all of us for months in advance, and the closer we got to it, the more intense and violent our practices became, the coaches egging us on with taunts aimed at kindling a kind of sectarian hatred. "Try throwing a block like that when we play Junior High," they'd say. "You'll get your head ripped off and shoved up your ass. Is that what you want? Well, all right, then. Suck it up!"

After the last practice leading up to the scrimmage in my eighth-grade year, our head coach, Sean Reilly, called the team together and gave us a speech about pride. It was the usual stuff: pride doesn't take plays off, pride never backs down, and so forth. Afterward, Coach Reilly invited me, as one of the team captains, to lead the team in prayer. "Lord," I remember beginning the prayer, "please protect us from injury and help us to play our best." But then the fire the coaches had been kindling in us all week took over, and I finished the prayer with these words: "And above all, Lord, HELP US TO KILL OUR ENEMIES!"

"No, no, no," Coach Reilly said, shaking his head. "Rebein, what *in the hell* are you saying? Have you gone nuts?"

After all the buildup, the scrimmage itself turned out to be something of a letdown. We more than held our own against our cross-town rivals, but the victory was tainted by the fact that several of their best players, including their leading ball carrier and most feared linebacker, were held out of the scrimmage as punishment for breaking team rules against smoking and drinking.

Had we won or lost? It was impossible to say. We finished that season with a perfect 5–0 record and went on to add a couple of tournament championships in basketball as well. But looking back on it all today, I don't recall any of these victories with the vividness with which I still see that single, ambiguous scrimmage. It was supposed to be the win that defined us, proving once and for all that we were worthy to represent our families and school—indeed, Catholicism itself. But in the end, all that was denied us. And for what—a pack of cigarettes and a couple of beers? How, I wondered, could the God I had been taught to know allow something like that to happen?

The idea that I would one day leave Sacred Heart to take my place in the wider world didn't really sink in for me until the middle of seventh grade, when Father Sloan began to visit our religion class to help us in our preparations for Confirmation. Father Sloan was what my classmates and I considered a "cool" priest. He was young and bearded, listened to rock music (Fleetwood Mac, not John Denver), and still drove the rusted-out van he had owned as a seminarian. For this reason, we probably took what Father Sloan had to say a little more seriously than we took the words of Monsignor Husman and the older priests.

"Confirmation is the last of the Sacraments of Initiation," Father Sloan told us. "But it's also the beginning of your adult lives in the church. You need to think about that and do a little soul-searching as we get closer to the ceremony."

"Soul-searching?" I asked, for this was not a term I had encountered before. "What do you mean by 'soul-searching'?"

"Well, correct me if I'm wrong, but you were a baby when you were baptized, and only six or seven years old at First Communion," Father explained. "You really didn't have the opportunity to choose those sacraments; instead, they were chosen for you by your parents and teachers. Confirmation is different."

"Are you saying we can choose *not* to be confirmed?" I asked. "No more studying or filling out all these workbooks? Is that what you're saying?"

"Well, it's certainly not something I recommend," Father answered. "But yes. Ultimately, the decision to be confirmed has to come from you. It has to come from *here*"—and with this he tapped himself above the heart—"otherwise, what's the point?"

No doubt these questions seemed fairly obvious and tame to someone such as Father Sloan, who had spent the better part of a decade turning them over in his head while studying to be a priest. But to me, at thirteen, they seemed radical and without precedent. Up to that point, I had never really questioned the Catholic Church or my place in it. Insofar as I had thought about it at all, it was with the sort of closed, circular reasoning that always brought me back to the same place from which I had departed only moments before.

What are you?

Catholic.

Why?

Because I go to Sacred Heart.

Why do you go to Sacred Heart?

Because I'm a Rebein. All of the Dodge City Rebeins go to Sacred Heart.

Why?

Because we're Catholic . . .

For reasons very similar to these, I went to Mass and confession, said the rosary, served as an altar boy at weddings and funerals, kneeled for hours before a glittering monstrance during the Forty Hours of Adoration, and so on. The idea of questioning any of this had never occurred to me. Of course, it was not as though I hadn't entertained doubts about certain aspects of Catholicism. For example, I hated and dreaded going to confession, viewing the entire ordeal as a kind of fear-inducing exercise designed to keep me up nights worrying about being run over by a bus before I'd had an opportunity to confess having thoroughly perused the December issue of *Playboy*. And far from having deepened my experience of the Mass, the three years I'd spent as an altar boy had only served to expose me to certain Oz-is-revealed realities such as holy water drawn from a tap, priestly vestments with ketchup and mustard stains, plastic bags of unconsecrated hosts with the words *Made in Cleveland* stamped on the label, and so on. However, none of this seriously shook my faith, for the simple reason that I had never once thought of Catholicism *as* a faith. It was instead a kind of genetic or geographical destiny, like red hair or being born to root for the Chicago Cubs. Only now, here was Father Sloan with his hippie beard and sandals, telling me just the opposite: Catholicism was a choice, not a destiny. It was all on me now; I had to decide.

And so, for the first time in my life, I began to imagine an existence untouched by the lessons and requirements of the Catholic Church. No more avoiding meat on Fridays during Lent, or yawning through the whole of midnight Mass. No more getting up at six to serve at the seven o'clock Mass, then staying on to do the school Mass at eight o'clock as well. No more confessing my sins through an opaque screen while the priest on the other side mumbled or wheezed his benediction. No more of any of that. As an initial step in the experiment, I told my parents I'd rather go to Saturday evening Mass so I could sleep in on Sunday morning. But after going a few times, I found other things to do instead, such as playing basketball in the school parking lot or wandering down to Boot Hill to watch the cars cruising up and down Wyatt Earp Boulevard. "It's my choice not to go," I told myself. Emboldened, I stopped going to confession, too. Because we went only once a month, on a Friday after school, the feat was easily accomplished. Indeed, no one even noticed my absence. However, I noticed. Indeed,

I felt the same freedom and exhilaration I'd felt the first time I skipped out on Mass. Soon I began to wonder if maybe I wasn't cut out to be a Catholic after all. I mean, if it really was my choice, then why not go ahead and make it?

The problem, of course, was that to make this decision meant publicly opting out of Confirmation, and that was a difficult thing to imagine, let alone act upon. Weeks went by and I did nothing. I continued to skip Mass most Saturday nights, but I still went five days a week with my class at school, where I also attended religion class and continued my preparations for Confirmation. Living this way, I began to feel like a fraud. I was living a lie, I told myself. Soon I would have to talk to someone about my crisis of faith.

Whenever I imagined this scene taking place, I always cast Father Sloan in the role of confessor. We would share a cup of coffee in his office in the rectory, and I would slowly outline for him my newfound reasons for not believing. The conversation would take place on a lofty, almost philosophical level, and it would end with Father Sloan congratulating me on the way I had thought everything through.

"You're smarter than the rest of the kids in the school," he would say. "That's why you're wrestling with all these big questions while your classmates are just going through the motions."

The reality was very different. I had just served as altar boy at the funeral and graveside service of an elderly parishioner named Mr. Pearl, and Monsignor Husman and I were on the way home from the cemetery in his dark blue Oldsmobile. It was a gorgeous day in late March or early April, and Monsignor had the windows of the car rolled down to take in the warm air. Monsignor's eulogy of Mr. Pearl, as I remember it, had been rote in the extreme, little more than a catalogue of the dates on which Mr. Pearl had received this or that sacrament. Baptized in infancy, he had attended Sacred Heart in the early days of its existence, making his First Communion and Confirmation there before going on to a life that included the sacrament of Matrimony, the usual allotment of children, and God only knew how many Masses and confessions and rosaries. Only days before, he had been given Last Rites, the final sacrament it was possible to receive. This, Monsignor announced woodenly, was precisely the way life was supposed to be lived, and Mr. Pearl should be thought of as a powerful example to us all.

But I wondered, *What was the point of it all? What had living such a life gained Mr. Pearl in the end, beyond a few rote words delivered by a bored priest who only an hour later was whistling happily on his way home from the cemetery?* The more I thought about it, the more Monsignor's eulogy began to seem like a last straw of sorts, and before I even knew what I was doing, I heard myself saying something like, "Golly, it sure makes you wonder, doesn't it?"

"What does?" Monsignor asked without looking at me.

"I don't know," I said. "All this stuff about God. I mean, what's the point anyway?"

As soon as I had uttered the words, I knew it was a mistake. After all, this wasn't Father Sloan I was addressing. I could feel Monsignor stiffen in the seat beside me, as his white head slowly turned to take me in. "What did you say?" he asked, sounding annoyed.

"Nothing," I answered. "Forget it."

"No," Monsignor said, shaking his head. "What did you say?"

Taking a deep breath, I repeated it all pretty much the same way I had said it before. Monsignor waited until I had finished, then said in an irritated voice, as if I had just ruined an otherwise perfect day, "What nonsense. I hope you haven't been infecting your classmates with any of this. Have you?"

"No," I answered through gritted teeth. "I haven't."

"Well, good," he said. "See to it that you don't."

That was it. We drove the rest of the way in silence, and when we got back to Sacred Heart, I changed quickly out of my altar boy garb and rushed to join my class at recess. But for days afterward, I could think of little else but the botched scene with

Monsignor. *What nonsense. I hope you haven't been infecting your classmates with any of this. Have you?* Every time those words passed through my brain, I felt like screaming, or worse. *To hell with him,* I thought. *To hell with it all!*

I had more or less made up my mind to boycott Confirmation when, one day after track practice, I stuck around the gym to shoot baskets with my seventh-grade teacher, a tall, pockmarked New Yorker named Mr. Small. If there was anyone who would understand what I was going through at that time, I figured it had to be Mr. Small. Wasn't it Small who had offered to answer every question about sex we cared to ask him, no matter how down and dirty? Hadn't the man quoted Billy Joel to the effect that it was better to laugh with the sinners than cry with the saints, because the sinners were much more fun? Surely a little religious wobbling wouldn't faze him.

"I've been thinking," I remember saying. "I just don't think I can go through with this Confirmation thing. I mean, what's the point? It's all a crock anyway."

Here Small picked up his dribble and gave me one of his patented New York frowns. "Come on, Wob," he said in his thick New York accent. "Be serious."

"I *am* serious," I answered him. "Really—what's the point?"

At this, Small rolled his eyes in that cynical way he had, dribbled once to his left, and banked a long jumper off the glass. "You want the point, Wob?" he asked. "All right, I'll give you the point. Your friends are expecting you to do it, and they're not the only ones. What about your mudder? What's she ever done to you to deserve this?"

Although it shouldn't have, the question took me completely by surprise. My mother? What did she have to do with any of this? Of course, a second later, I could see it all with perfect clarity—the cathedral packed to the gills, the bishop in attendance, everyone in my class making their way down the aisle, their mothers and fathers smiling proudly, camera bulbs exploding from every corner of the church. Everyone but my mom and dad, that is.

"I guess I see what you mean," I said, rebounding Small's shot and rifling the ball back to him where he waited at the top of the key.

"I thought you would, Wob," he answered with a craggy smile. "I thought you would."

On May 14, 1978, I dutifully participated in my own Confirmation. The following year, I graduated from Sacred Heart and moved over to the dreaded junior high, where, as advertised, there were thugs and drugs and sexual favors traded in broom closets off the main hallway. No learning of any kind went on that I could see, and nobody cared what I did so long as it didn't cause the fire alarms to go off or require a visit to the school by the police.

In response to this chaos, I concentrated on sports and took a lot of art classes, which weren't offered at Sacred Heart. Sometimes, navigating those hallways where no lines were ever formed and the noise was so loud it hurt my ears, I would catch sight of one of my former Catholic school chums, and we would trade looks of wide-eyed amusement. We were appalled by almost everything we saw, but it was not as if, given the choice, we would have gone back to Sacred Heart. The way we saw it, we had been delivered from all that and were free now—or at least as free as kids like us would ever be.

Dragging Wyatt Earp

Hear the words *Dodge City, Kansas,* these days and you're apt to think, depending on your age, either of a moribund 1970s TV series—the wildly fictitious *Gunsmoke,* featuring Miss Kitty, Festus, and Marshal Matt Dillon—or else of a favorite phrase of screen hacks and gleeful, road-tripping frat boys: *Let's get the hell out of Dodge!* Few are the souls who would hear the town's name and think of the *real* Dodge City, self-proclaimed "Cowboy Capital of the World," with its beef packing plants and used car lots and the tired tones of boosterism ("Come Grow with Us!") emanating from its chamber of commerce. To know that Dodge, you'd have to have crossed southwestern Kansas in a car, an experience road-weary travelers have been known to compare to crossing the ocean by sail. Either that or, like me, you'd have to be from there.

It's been twenty years now since I escaped the place, and in that time, the real Dodge City, with its dry riverbed and red brick streets, grain elevators casting shadows across an empty downtown, the air filled with dust or tinged with a fecal tang blown in from the feedlots, the Dodge of the Red Demons and the Conqs (short for Conquistadors) and the now-defunct St. Mary of the Plains Cavaliers, of the dying mall called Village Square, the scarred but still functional South Drive-In, the cheesy tourist traps (Boot Hill and Front Street, Home of Stone, Kansas Teachers' Hall of Fame), none of them worth the drive and not meant to be, the Dodge of the diseased Dutch elm and incessant, driving wind, with its country club and tacquerias, its chiropractic clinics and failing farm implement dealerships, and its Gene's Heartland Foods that used to be a Safeway that used to be the hospital where I was born . . . *that* Dodge City almost ceased to exist for me, having been replaced in my mind by the Dodge of legend and myth, the so-called Queen of the Cowtowns, the Wickedest Little City in America, the Bibulous Babylon of the Frontier.

Almost, but not quite.

For while I confess to a weakness for tales of the Old West, particularly those having to do with my hometown's sordid past, in most important respects—in memory, imagination, all the infinitesimal allegiances of identity—I remain tied to that other Dodge, *my* Dodge, the one that raised me up and forgave my feeble sins and never once asked for a single thing in return except that I leave and find my future elsewhere.

For teenagers suffering the boredom of the Cowboy Capital circa 1980, the only thing to do at night, so we all said, was to "drag Wyatt Earp." By this we did not mean, as the image would suggest, that we would pull the nineteenth-century lawman through the streets by his boot heels, but only that we would cruise up and down Wyatt Earp Boulevard in our beat-up Chevrolets and hand-me-down Buicks, searching for that elusive bit of excitement that always seemed to exist just outside of our reach. Wyatt Earp, to us, was not a person but a *place,* a mile-long ribbon of asphalt that stretched from Boot Hill on the east to the Dodge House on the west, containing in that brief space all of our teeming and awkward adolescence, our collective longings and flirtations and our often ridiculous mistakes, few of which we had to pay for in any meaningful way.

Dragging Wyatt Earp was a ritual and a clearly demarcated rite of passage, one that began at fourteen or fifteen, the years when most of us were issued our first driver's licenses, and ended two or three years later, when the pool halls and beer joints and lakeside keg parties began to absorb us. Had we been city kids, we'd have been hanging out at the mall or the cineplex. But we weren't city kids, and Dodge was a suburb of nowhere, hundreds of mostly tedious miles from Dallas, Denver, or Kansas

City, and there was much that we would never do or see before the age of nineteen or twenty. But we could drink and we could drive, both at early ages and in plain sight of the police. A kind of unwritten law had been established long ago.

I can recall, at sixteen or seventeen, wheeling into the Kwik Shop at Twelfth and Wyatt Earp and emerging five minutes later with a six-pack of Coors cradled in my arm like a football. Often the person selling me the beer knew exactly who I was, who my father and brothers were, what position I played on the high school basketball team. Sometimes there'd be a cop car in the parking lot when I came out, two sheriff's deputies sitting side by side with their elbows jutting out open windows. I'd nod to them as I ambled past with my illicit cargo, and they'd nod right back in that slow, calculated manner of police everywhere.

"You be careful now, you hear?"

"Yes, sir," I'd answer.

Once on Earp, the routine rarely varied. The official speed limit was thirty-five miles an hour, but as with the drinking age, we regarded this as more of a suggestion than an actual law. Either you went fifteen or you went fifty, depending on your style and purpose, the level of gas in your tank, the amount of beer or Jack Daniels or peppermint schnapps you'd consumed. Racing from one light to the next was not unheard of, but neither was it a regular occurrence. A pecking order had been established long before, in seventh or eighth grade, so what was the point? Dragging Wyatt Earp was about killing time; it was about hanging out and hooking up, growing up and throwing up (indeed, in the teen vernacular of Dodge City circa 1980, to "erp" was to vomit, usually by hanging one's head out the door of a moving car); it was about chasing dreams and bursting at the seams and endlessly rehearsing for that preordained day when we, too, would get the hell out of Dodge, never to return.

Dodge City in 1876 was a quintessential western boomtown, a nexus for cash and cattle where overlords such as the legendary Shanghai Pierce sold their massive herds at a profit and immediately paid off their hired underlings, most of them young Texans away from home for the first time. To say that the merchants of Dodge City saw these greenhorns coming would be an understatement of epic proportions. In a piece published in the *Dodge City Times* in the spring of 1878, editor Nicholas Klaine made no bones about the anticipation with which "this delectable city of the plains" awaited the return of the cattle trade, with its "countless herds" and "hordes of bipeds." As many as 1,500 of these "bipeds" might hit town in a single season, and as Klaine, licking his chops, pointed out, Dodge City was the single "source from which the great army of the herder and driver is fed": "This 'cattle village' and far-famed 'wicked city' is decked in gorgeous attire in preparation for the long horn. Like the sweet harbinger of spring, the boot black came, he of white and he of black. Next the barber 'with his lather and shave.' Too, with all that go to make up the busy throng of life's faithful fever, come the Mary Magdalenes, 'selling their souls to whoever'll buy.' There is 'high, low, jack, and game,' all adding to the great expectation so important an event brings about."

If there was a problem in all this, a glitch, so to speak, in an otherwise flawless business plan, it was the town's tendency to erupt in periodic bouts of profit-draining violence. Ordinances against public intoxication and the carrying of firearms in the city limits were duly composed and promulgated, but enforcing them was another matter. That required the deft touch of a man like Wyatt Earp, who had honed his skills as a peace officer in the cowtowns of Ellsworth and Wichita and was more than ready to employ them in Dodge, too—provided, of course, the price was right.

The epicenter of my teen years was the parking lot below Boot Hill Museum, a rectangle of concrete the size of a football field that on any given night contained the same tribes and anthropologically interesting subgroups as the high school—jocks, cheerleaders, potheads, Future Farmers of America—the only difference being that here one leaned against the polished hood of a car instead of against a locker. The same atmosphere of boredom, of stoically doing time, obtained in both places. If someone had asked our parents why they allowed us to openly drink alcohol in a parking lot in the middle of town, they probably would have said, "At least we know where they are. At least they're *safe*." Yet what irony, that this, the place we gathered most nights to gossip, pose, and drink beer, bore a name synonymous the world over with sin and violent death. The phrases *dead line, red light district,* and *die with your boots on* all originated here, as did the legends of Wyatt Earp and Bat Masterson, Doc Holliday and Big Nose Kate Elder, Mysterious Dave Mather and Squirrel Tooth Alice.

Did we know? Did we care? But what's the use of asking: we were teenagers, after all. It would have taken something considerably more than mere history to impress us. In the middle of the parking lot was a large cage, perhaps ten feet square, made of two-by-fours and chicken wire. Sometime before, so the story went, the parking lot had become so littered with our crushed beer cans that someone's dad or Eagle Scout older brother had been inspired to build the cage to hold the empties. I couldn't say now whether the story is true, but we certainly were proud of it at the time, and most weekends we possessed no higher ambition than to "fill the cage."

This was the kind of thing that mattered to us, not Wyatt Earp, not history.

Boot Hill parking lot was the place I took my first real girlfriend on our first real date. She was a cheerleader with ambitions to be crowned homecoming queen, and I was a jock suffering from the usual jock grandiosity. I can still recall what it felt like to make that slow, head-turning crawl through the cars parked at Boot Hill. You weren't an official couple until you'd run that gauntlet. Later, when the relationship began to crumble under the weight of its own importance, Boot Hill parking lot was also the place I would go late at night to cheat on this girlfriend (try to, at any rate), so secure was I in the knowledge that no one who saw me there would dare tell the secret. Like the French Quarter of New Orleans, Boot Hill possessed a strange, nearly magical ability to transform itself several times daily, from afternoon tourist haven to evening esplanade to late-night cruising ground; if the vibe reigning at any one time didn't suit, you could always come back later, and, like the weather on the high plains, it would be sure to have changed.

That world! Looking back, I don't see a series of clearly demarcated nights, but rather a blur, a collage. I see the pimpled faces of my friends, our bad haircuts and unfashionable clothes. I hear the over-amped music, Led Zeppelin, AC/DC, Kool and the Gang, Bob Seger. I smell the burned oil and rubber and gasoline and weed, recall the sickly sweet taste of Copenhagen and Skoal, Jack Daniels sipped from a wax cup, the sloppy kisses copped in cramped backseats, and the feel of tight jeans and no hat even in the winter and the stiff arms of my new letter jacket. I remember the roadside signs, McDonalds, Burger King, Pizza Hut, but also El Charro, Kirby's Western Store, OK Tire, Muddy Waters, El Matador. I remember the cars, especially the newer, faster ones with their space-age names (RX-7, 280Z) and the lovingly restored older models ('57 Chevy, '64 Mustang, '69 GTO). My own pride and joy was a dark green 1970 Firebird Formula 400, a huge, hulking beast with a chrome-studded engine, fat tires with raised white letters, and a six-speaker stereo system that cost more than the car itself.

Most of all, though, I remember the talk, the ceaseless posturing and bragging and trying on of ideas, the feeble put-downs and bad jokes and misty-eyed confessions, the sputtering declarations of love. As with teenagers everywhere, we existed in a bizarre, fog-bound realm in which the present was at once insufferable and all-important. The past did not exist at all, and when the subject of the future flared up, as it did periodically, we were quick to smother it in a series of outlandish predictions. We would win Daytona, take Hollywood by storm, run for the US Senate, earn our first million by the age of thirty, and so on. No plans for how we would accomplish these things were ever asked for, and none were given. Unlike our peers in the cities and the suburbs, we didn't sweat the details. We just believed.

What is it about growing up in a small town in the West that breeds such bravado, such innocence and blind faith? Was it our isolation? The vaunted self-reliance of the region? The fact that our parents and teachers praised us inordinately or that acceptance into any of the state's colleges was a fait accompli? Maybe, but I have another explanation: we were leaving. And not just for a year or five years, but forever. Like the region's cattle, wheat, and corn, we'd been raised for export, and most of us had learned this fact at about the same time we learned that Santa Claus was a fiction. Coming into this knowledge was both terrifying and liberating. It was like looking over the edge of a great abyss or knowing in advance the date of your own death. It steeled us and set us apart. And yet, for all that, there was no need for alarm or haste or even preparation. As far as we were concerned, the day of our departure would come of its own accord, just as morning would come, after a long night of dragging Wyatt Earp.

Other frontier lawmen might have been faster on the draw, better liars, more handsome and flamboyant—Wild Bill Hickok comes to mind in all of these categories—but none was better at handling drunks than Wyatt S. Earp.

According to newspaper articles on file at the Kansas Heritage Center, Wyatt Berry Stapp Earp was a deputy city marshal in Dodge City—a policeman, essentially—from May 1876 to October 1879, the height of the city's cowtown fame, during which time he earned a reputation as "one of the most efficient officers Dodge ever had," a cop with "a quiet way of taking the most desperate characters into custody."

What was this "quiet method" of Marshal Earp's? An item from the August 20, 1878, *Ford County Globe* sheds some light on the matter. "Another shooting affair occurred on the 'south side' Saturday night," the article begins. "It appears that one of the cow boys, becoming intoxicated and quarrelsome, undertook to take possession of the bar in the Comique. To this the bar keeper objected and a row ensued. Our policemen interfered and had some difficulty in handling their man. Several cattle men then engaged in the broil and in the excitement some of them were bruised on the head with six shooters."

Plainly put, during his stint with the Dodge City police, Wyatt Earp became known not for shooting his gun—a Colt .45 specially modified with an extended barrel almost a foot long (the infamous "Buntline Special")—but rather for using it to brain belligerent drunks. "If some obstreperous cowboy resisted arrest," Earp told his biographer, the fawning Stuart Lake, "a marshal could jerk his gun, bat him over the head, and end the argument." Earp had various names for this favorite ploy of his: "manhandling," "buffaloing," "bending a six-gun over a man's head." We moderns employ another term—excessive force—but in Earp's day it was thought that a cop who kept order without actually firing his gun was a very good cop indeed.

So much of what we think we know about Wyatt Earp turns out, on closer examination, to be false or misleading. Having studied the famous photographs, all of them in black and white, we naturally imagine a dark man, when by all reports Earp was a strawberry blond with blue eyes. Having seen the movies and TV shows, we imagine a big man, someone of the stature of John Wayne or, better yet, James Arness of *Gunsmoke* fame, when in truth Earp was rather slight, never weighing more than 160 pounds. Having read the pulps, we picture a classic gunslinger, a man standing alone at high noon, but as a cowtown cop, Earp worked almost exclusively at night and in tandem with other police, who remembered him not as a "quick draw" or "crack shot" but as an accomplished brawler, a bare-knuckles fighter of such skill and tenacity that fellow cop Bat Masterson, later a New York sportswriter, was reminded of none other than the legendary Jim Corbett. "I doubt if there was a man in the West who could whip [Wyatt] in a rough-and-tumble fight," Masterson wrote.

As for the self-doubt and scruples Hollywood prefers in its cinematic marshals, apparently Wyatt Earp wasn't much troubled by these. The testimony of those who knew him best describes a dour, supremely confident man who inspired fear in his enemies and loyalty in his friends. Earp was calm, experienced, and methodical, and perhaps most important of all, he did not drink. Add to this the fact, as one biographer has it, that the young Earp "grew up in the same pro-union, Republican, progressive, antislavery atmosphere that spawned Abraham Lincoln," and the portrait is complete. The man Dodge City's saloon owners hired to keep the peace in the Wicked City was neither a hero nor a saint but rather a detached, seasoned, and somewhat sadistic teetotaler who was good with his fists and didn't much care for the Rebel scum he was charged with arresting on a nightly basis.

For his work in Dodge, Earp drew a salary of one hundred dollars a month, plus a two-dollar bonus for every arrest made. According to Stuart Lake, one of Earp's innovations as a Dodge City marshal was to pool these bonuses and share them among all the cops on the force—provided the arrests were made without shots being fired. "I figured that if the cowboys were man-handled and heaved into the caboose every time they showed in town with guns on, or cut loose in forbidden territory, they'd come to time quicker than if we kept them primed for gunplay," Earp recalled.

Earp's idea—to kill no one but collect plenty of bounties from buffaloed drunks—worked like a charm from first to last. "We winged a few tough customers who insisted on shooting, but none of the victims died," he recalled. "On the other hand, we split seven or eight hundred dollars in bounties each month. That meant some three hundred arrests every thirty days, and as practically every prisoner heaved into the caboose was thoroughly buffaloed in the process, we made quite a dent in the cowboy conceit."

Dent indeed! Earp's calculation here is as chilling as his methods were brutal, yet a century and a half later, it's difficult to argue with his basic premise, which counted a rap on the skull as a lesser evil than a bullet in the brain.

Admired by those whose pockets he helped fill, hated by those whose skulls he bruised, Wyatt Earp was the greatest bouncer the West ever knew.

Of all the nights I spent cruising the strip that bears Earp's name, only one stands apart. It was a hot night the summer before my junior year of high school, and a friend and I had spent it at the South Drive-In, reclining in beach chairs and sipping at a twelve-pack of smuggled-in Coors. I don't remember what movie played that night or if it was any good. I don't even recall how many beers I consumed or in what span of time I consumed them. All I really remember is that in comparison to other nights that came both before and after this one, I wasn't particularly drunk. Certainly I had no business behind the wheel of a car, but that, like so many others, was a lesson I had yet to learn.

The movie over, we tossed the beach chairs into the back of the Firebird and bounced out of the lunar landscape of the theater. "Wanna drag Earp a few times?" I asked.

"Yeah, why not," answered my friend, who in years to come would earn a degree in nuclear engineering and circumnavigate the globe in a Cold War sub.

We crossed the dry Arkansas at Second Avenue, not far from where the Spanish conquistador Coronado had crossed more than four hundred years before, and merged quickly into the night traffic on West Wyatt Earp. What were we thinking? Where were we going? It's all lost now, like the motivations of the men and women who stare back at us, bug-eyed, from nineteenth-century daguerreotypes. Approaching Boot Hill, we craned our heads to the right, cataloguing in an instant all of the cars parked there. Vaguely, as though attempting to see through a fog, I recall a disturbance in my rearview mirror, something only partially blocked by the beach chairs piled haphazardly in the backseat. What was it? A flash of headlights? The street-light behind us turning from yellow to red? Whatever it was, I veered sharply into the right-hand lane, sideswiping a carload of Utah tourists. The Firebird shot forward, jumped a curb, and narrowly missed a phone pole before coming to rest next to a chain-link fence.

"What the hell!" my friend howled. The paper cup he'd been using as a spittoon had overturned in his lap, filling the car with a sharp, wintergreen smell.

"You all right?" I asked, blinking at the red lights aglow in the car's dash.

"Well, I guess," my friend said.

Moments later, a city patrolman who'd witnessed the entire episode rolled to a stop behind us, lights silently flashing.

What happened next could only have happened in that time and place, or so I've come to believe. With the whole of Boot Hill parking lot looking on, my friend and I were pulled from the Firebird and deposited in the back of the patrolman's copper-and-cream squad car, there to sweat the minutes while he calmed the tourists and sent them on their way. Afterward, the patrolman, whose name I've forgotten, took up an aggressive position, legs spread wide, behind the Firebird's license plate, and began writing tickets.

"Can you walk heel to toe?" my friend asked, attempting a joke. "Can you recite the alphabet backwards?"

Scared, my throat dry from the Copenhagen I'd swallowed in the crash, I said nothing at all in response, but only sat there watching as the patrolman closed his aluminum ticket box and began a bow-legged amble back to where we waited.

"Get out," he ordered, opening my door.

I scrambled from the backseat of the squad car, my friend following, and together we lined up in the glare of the car's head-lights. By then there were twenty or more people looking on, most of them across the road from us and unable to hear what was said.

"Think you can drive that heap of yours?" the patrolman asked, handing me the stack of tickets he'd written.

I nodded, still too scared to say a word.

"All right, then," he said, shaking his head. "Straight home, fellas. No detours. You hear?"

"Yes, sir," I managed to say.

As we sped away from there, my friend performed a quick inventory of the tickets. "Reckless driving, failure to signal. . . . What is this, your lucky day?"

"I guess so," I said.

Before work the following Monday, I walked into the county courthouse and paid the tickets in full, using money I'd been saving for college. The total damage was something on the order of four hundred dollars, but I paid it gladly.

Two years later, I packed my bags and headed east on Highway 56, reversing the outbound path of the old Santa Fe Trail. I can still hear the throaty roar of the Firebird as I opened all four barrels of the carburetor. Trust me when I tell you that I worshiped every inch of that ridiculous beast, and yet, six months later, with little forethought and no real regrets, I walked onto a used car lot in North Lawrence, Kansas, and traded straight across for a boxy, puke-green 1975 Volvo. So do we shed our adolescent selves and venture forth into a larger, less forgiving world.

Wyatt Earp left Dodge City for Tombstone, Arizona, in September 1879. In Earp's words, "Dodge's edge was getting dull." In 1885, the wooden shanties of Front Street, the model for a thousand Hollywood sets, burned to the ground in a series of freakish fires. The following winter delivered a devastating storm, the great blizzard of 1886, which decimated herds across the West, bankrupted most of the big ranches, and brought the so-called Cattle Kingdom to its knees. But even before the arrival of fire and ice, the writing was already on the wall. "There are silent but irresistible forces at work to regenerate Dodge City," the *Topeka Capital* reported in 1885. "The passage of the Texas cattle bill, the defeat of the trail bill and the rapid settlement of the country south and southwest of Dodge, have destroyed the place as a cattle town. The cowboy must go, and with him will go the gamblers, the courtesans, the desperadoes and the saloons."

With the good-time people gone away, sodbusters, precursors of my own humble ancestors, moved in and broke up the prairie into massive, monotonous wheat farms. With them came the temperance unions that had already tamed the eastern half of the state. And so the town turned its back on its sordid past and accepted a sober if somewhat boring future. When Front Street was rebuilt after the fires of 1885, the work was done in brick—a safer, more permanent choice than wood. Fifteen years later, on the cusp of a new century, the place had changed so much that the editors of the *Globe-Republican* proudly declared the birth of a "New Dodge City," no longer a place of "high carnival," where "rapturous lewdness and bawdiness held sway," but rather a city "clothed in her right mind," "a paragon of virtue, sobriety and industry."

There's an undeniable sadness to all this that resonates even today—the circus gone, the party over, the days of debauched glory all in the past. Innocence gives way to experience, the child grows to adulthood, the young colt goes into harness and is made to pull the wagon of duty. Inevitably, a kind of nostalgia sets in. When word spread that Warner Brothers was planning a movie based on the city's lurid past, a delegation of old-timers and chamber of commerce types traveled to Hollywood to invite Jack Warner to stage the film's premiere in Dodge. Photographs of this 1939 event look surreal, with fifty thousand fans crowding the tracks of the Santa Fe depot to await the arrival of Errol Flynn, Jean Parker, and Humphrey Bogart. Twenty years later, in 1958, a replica of the original Front Street was built on a slope below Boot Hill, and the road running below it, formerly Chestnut Street, was renamed Wyatt Earp Boulevard. In 1970, brick Front Street fell to the wrecking ball to make room for more off-street parking and the widening of Wyatt Earp to accommodate the likes of McDonalds and Kentucky Fried Chicken. Thus did Front Street, upon which, as Zane

Grey famously wrote, more frontier history was enacted than anywhere else in the West, become a fast-food corridor and the latest outpost of Auto Zone and Applebee's.

Last summer, I returned to Dodge City on the occasion of my parents' fiftieth wedding anniversary, rolling into town from the east behind the wheel of a loaded-to-the-gills SUV in the backseat of which my son and daughter watched *Shrek 2* on their portable flat-screen TV. Driving up Wyatt Earp to Fourteenth Street, I was amused to see that the Kwik Shop where I once bought beer was now Doc Holliday Liquors. Across the street, on the site of an old Sinclair station, stood Wyatt Earp Liquors. Since the beef packing plants moved in twenty years ago, the town has become more western and Hispanic, the airwaves full of country music, programming in Spanish, advertisements for the annual Dodge City Days Roundup Rodeo. This, too, is my Dodge City, although I do not yet know it half as well as I would like to.

In the years since I got the hell out of Dodge, I've lived in three different states and two foreign countries. I've married, fathered children and a career, and have seen a handful of dreams come true, while others have died on the vine, despite all my efforts to keep them alive. To return home after years away is at best a bittersweet thing. It is to encounter ghosts at every stoplight and corner—ghosts of what once was, as well as ghosts of what might have been.

As I turned north on Fourteenth Street, just as I had as a kid heading home after a long night of dragging Wyatt Earp, I was reminded of what that policeman told my friend and me all those years ago.

"Straight home, fellas. No detours."

But it's all detours after a while.

The family of Joseph and Clara Rebein, Ellinwood, Kansas, circa 1898. The author's grandfather, Anthony Rebein, born in Ellinwood in 1888, stands between his parents in the middle of the second row.

The author's father, William Rebein, in front of the family farmhouse northwest of Dodge City, circa 1940.

Bill, Tony, and Harold Rebein, circa 1950.

The author's mother, Patricia McDonald Rebein, as a teenager in Wichita, Kansas.

Patricia and Bill Rebein on the farm in the early days of their marriage.

Bill Rebein (*far right*) with the modified jalopy he built with his friend John Bauer (*far left*). Seated between them is Cecil Maupin, Jr., a rival race driver and the owner of Maupin Truck Parts.

The Rebein boys, Christmas 1964, three years before the move to town. *Clockwise from top:* Dave (holding the author), Alan, Steve, Tom, Joe.

The author and his youngest brother, Paul, outfitted as gunslingers, circa 1971.

Bill Rebein accepting an award in his B & B Auto Parts uniform.

The "bloated mansion" as it looked in 1983, fifteen years after the move to town. In the driveway is the author's 1970 Firebird Formula 400, car of choice for countless nights of "dragging Wyatt Earp."

The author with his wife, Alyssa, and their children, Ria and Jake, at a family wedding in Dodge City.

The author with Cuba in Owl Rock pasture, Lazy R Ranch, fourteen miles northeast of Dodge City.

PART II
THE COUNTRY

The Greatest Game Country on Earth

> [Hunting] . . . is such a universal and
> impassioned sport that it belongs in the
> repertory of the purest forms of human
> happiness.
>
> —Jose Ortega y Gasset

Before I knew anything of his Civil War record or iconic
death at the Battle of the Little Bighorn, I knew George Armstrong Custer as a hunter on the plains of Kansas. This knowledge was conferred on me in fourth or fifth grade, during a field
trip my classmates and I took to Old Fort Dodge, a few miles
east of our dusty and denuded hometown. After pointing out
the windblown parade ground and squat, stone barracks, our
tour guide, a man so consumed by wrinkles it seemed to me he
might have known Custer personally, led us into Sutler's Store
(or was it the building known as the Custer House even though
Custer himself never lived there?) and stood us before a grainy
photograph of the general. In the picture, taken in the autumn
of 1868, a bearded Custer, rifle in hand, stands before the open
flap of a conical Selby tent, a pair of stately greyhounds teth-
ered at his feet.

"What did he have those dogs for?" I remember asking.

"Why, hunting, of course," the old man replied. "They
say the general was a regular fool when it came to running
those dogs."

"What did he hunt?" I asked, excited. "Pheasants, I bet."

"No, he didn't hunt *pheasants*," the old man laughed derisively. "Pheasants come from *China*, son. There wasn't no

pheasants in Kansas back then. Let me tell you something about those days . . ."

By then, however, I was listening with at most half my being. The other half had been swallowed whole by certain details in the old-timey photo—the dogs in particular. Wiry and intense, their bodies little more than a blur, they appeared ready to jump out of their skins any second. I recognized that feeling all too well. Like them, I couldn't sit still for more than a few minutes at a time. I wanted to be *free,* to grow up fast and go wherever I pleased, whenever I pleased. Hunting, to me, seemed like the perfect way to achieve that freedom. Indeed, hearing the old man drone on about Custer and his glory days in Kansas, I couldn't help but imagine that it was me out there on those rolling, treeless plains, confined by nothing but the scope of my dreams and the size of my bravado.

I got my first BB gun, a lever-action Daisy, when I was seven years old. Within hours, the alley to the side of my house was awash in broken glass. Soon I graduated to other targets. A block to the south stood a Mormon church whose bell tower and eaves had been invaded by pigeons. I longed to put the fear of God into these birds, but the Daisy could do little more than annoy them. Then an older boy from the neighborhood loaned me his CO_2-powered pellet gun. "Now you're in business," he said. I set up in a tree behind the church and began taking potshots at the pigeons as they flew past me in broad, sweeping circles. I didn't manage to hit a single one, but a couple of weeks later, I overheard my parents discussing in loud, disgusted voices the "idiot teenager" who had inexplicably "shot up the windows of the Mormon church."

"I hope *you* won't grow up to do anything that stupid," my mother said, as I sneaked from the room.

When I was nine, following a long campaign of whining, I was given an archery set. My father set up a wall of hay bales in the yard next to the alley, affixed a paper target to it, and

walked off shaking his head. However, as my mother had predicted, I soon grew bored with the repetitive task of shooting
and retrieving the arrows. I had not begged for the archery set
all those months in order to become . . . an archer. I wanted to
hunt. I remember asking one of the teachers at my school (he
was from New York City, but that's another story) what sort
of game the Cheyennes and Sioux had stalked with their bows
and arrows.

"Oh, you know," the teacher answered breezily. "Buffalo,
antelope, fish . . ."

"Fish?" I asked.

"Sure," the teacher said, performing a lazy pantomime of
an Indian walking a creek bed with a drawn bow at the ready.

After school that day, I littered the side yard with soda and
beer cans, then tiptoed among them, letting my arrows fly. When
I thought I had practiced enough, I hopped on my Schwinn and
headed for the Arkansas River, a mile away. The closer I got,
the more I heard the whine of what sounded to me like boat
engines. *That's all right,* I told myself. *I'll stay close to the bank,
away from the traffic . . .* Then I emerged from Wright Park and
climbed the north bank of the river and saw to my dismay that
the river was dry—no water at all, not even a standing pool,
just sand, a tangle of flood-control wire, and a swarm of dirt
bikes and dune buggies.

I stood there a long moment, chiding myself. The part of
the Arkansas that ran through Dodge City had been drained
long ago by diversion projects upstream in Colorado. We had
covered all this in school, but in my excitement I had forgotten. Then, as my disappointment began to turn to anger, a
large, collarless, marmalade-colored cat emerged from the
dusty weeds lining the riverbank. On impulse, I drew an arrow
from the quiver on my back and pulled the bowstring taut. I
thought long and hard about killing that cat, but in the end I
couldn't bring myself to do it. Instead, I just stood there and
watched as he slinked past me on his way to the park's overflowing garbage cans.

At one time, that stretch of the Arkansas River near Dodge City was said to be the greatest game country on earth. At least that's the designation given to it by the pioneer Robert M. Wright, who arrived in southwestern Kansas in the 1850s and saw the country in its glory. "There were wonderful herds of buffalo, antelope, deer, elk and wild horses," Wright recalls in his 1913 memoir *Dodge City: The Cowboy Capital and the Great Southwest*. "There were big gray wolves and coyotes by the thousand. . . . There were also black and cinnamon bears, wild cats and mountain lions," as well as "the cunning little prairie dog—millions of them." Along the creeks and streams were "a great number of water-fowl and amphibious animals, such as the otter, beaver, muskrat, weasel, and mink," to say nothing of "ducks, geese, swans, brants, pelicans, [and] cranes." "It was a poor day," Wright concludes, "or a poor hunter who could not kill a hundred ducks and geese in a day, and sometimes several hundred were killed in a day." As for wild turkeys and quail, "there was no end to them. Their number were countless; one could not estimate them. Indeed, I am almost ashamed to state how many I have seen . . ."

This problem of counting plagued Wright, who was a storekeeper by trade and liked to keep an accurate tab on things. However, in this case, the task was all but impossible. "I have indeed traveled through buffaloes along the Arkansas river for two hundred miles, almost one continuous herd," Wright remembers. "When, after nightfall, they came to the river, particularly when it was in flood, their immense numbers, in their headlong plunge, would make you think, by the thunderous noise, that they had dashed all the water from the river."

It was to this magnificent game country that George Armstrong Custer reported for duty in the autumn of 1866. According to his wife, Elizabeth, the general had at first hoped to be stationed at Fort Garland in the mountains of Colorado, where the hunting was said to be excellent. But when he got off the train at Fort Riley in central Kansas, he promptly fell in love, declaring the plains region, with his usual flair for overstatement, "the fairest and richest portion of the national domain." At Fort Riley, Custer made the acquaintance of a number of legendary hunters and guides, Wild Bill Hickok among them. From Hickok, Custer freely appropriated the long, flowing hair and flamboyant buckskin attire of the plainsman. The general had always been one to look the part, but now he outdid himself, going so far as to equip himself with a Bowie knife and a pair of "ivory-handled revolvers of the large size," just like Wild Bill's.

The way Custer saw it, service on the plains of Kansas promised to be a safari of sorts, a carefree romp in the course of which a man might expect to bag multitudinous amounts of trophy game. As for the pesky Cheyennes and unruly Sioux, Custer expected (wrongly, it turned out) that campaigning against these tribes would be more of a sport than an act of war, resembling "the course of a . . . sportsman who, with a well-trained pointer or setter, thoroughly ranges and beats the ground in search of his coveted game."

To this end, Custer brought with him to Kansas, in addition to Elizabeth, several thoroughbred horses and a pack of English greyhounds.

In the late summer of 1976, I toted my brother Alan's J. C. Higgins model 12 gauge around the parking lot of the National Guard Armory one Saturday afternoon, thus passing the Kansas Safe Hunter program and earning the right to buy my first hunting license. I was twelve years old. In the fall of that year, I began hunting every weekend with a school chum, Charlie George, and his two older brothers, Bob and Pat. The George boys were known across three counties for their fanatical love of hunting. Behind the family's car dealership in South Dodge was a large kennel that housed a succession of shorthaired pointers and hyperactive spaniels. However, these dogs rarely saw any action after Charlie and I started hunting. Why go to the trouble of training a bird dog when you could treat your much-younger kid brother and his overly enthusiastic friend as if *they were dogs*, sending them out before you to beat the brush and retrieve downed birds? We got to carry guns, too, of course. But given the speed of the action and Bob's and Pat's quick fingers on the trigger, these were largely ornaments. Only in the final weeks of the season did Bob and Pat begin to hold their fire long enough for Charlie and me to get off shots of our own.

The first bird I ever brought down was in a snow-covered patch of milo stubble a few miles west of Dodge. I nearly stepped on it—that's how hard that rooster sat before exploding into the air directly in front of me. Startled, my heart climbing into my throat, I shouldered the too-big gun, swung through the arc of the pheasant's flight, and squeezed the trigger. The bird's furiously pounding wings halted in midair, and its limp body fell from the sky like something dropped from a low-flying airplane. By the time it made contact with the frozen ground, I was already running through the knee-high stubble, gun held out before me, commando-style.

A trail of blood led me to where the pheasant lay in the snow. I felt the warmth of the still-live body in my hands, the way its spurred feet fought against me, the terrible, unblinking eyes. As I had been taught to do, I quickly wrung the pheasant's neck—once, twice, three times around—until the kicking ceased and the eyes closed. A feeling of responsibility and awe passed through me. The person I had been only moments before was gone forever, replaced by a being that was at once higher and lower than my former self. As if to mark this change in me, I held the dead bird aloft for my companions to admire.

"Nice shot," Pat observed drily. "Next time, though, you might want to let that bird get a little farther out, otherwise there won't be anything left to eat but a mouthful of lead."

"I got him, though, didn't I?" I countered.

"That you did," Pat acknowledged. "That you did."

Two years later, Charlie and I turned fourteen, and the State of Kansas saw fit to issue us our first driver's licenses. From then on, we mostly hunted by ourselves. From dawn on Saturday until dusk on Sunday, we roamed the countryside south and west of town in Charlie's dilapidated Chevy Blazer. We were ambush artists, descending with blitzkrieg speed on a series of five- or six-acre weed patches. In a typical day of hunting, we might cover several hundred miles and visit forty or fifty such patches, all of which had names in our growing lexicon of place—Balderson Corners, Eckles, Cimarron Feeders, Protection, and so on.

That this land no longer qualified as the greatest game country on earth would have been obvious even from thirty thousand feet. The endless expanse of grass Robert Wright had known was gone, replaced by a monotonous grid of wheat fields and irrigation circles and craggy pastures enclosed in barbed wire. The herds of buffalo and elk were gone, too, replaced by hybridized cattle and tick-infested deer. In the place of wolves, there were coyotes. In the place of plovers and prairie chickens, there were pheasants. But to us, that part of Kansas still qualified as a paradise of sorts. Vast and largely depopulated, the roads unmarked (and, in many cases, unnamed), uniform in appearance, yet full of a million meaningful variations, it was still capable of producing in the person who came to know it well a kind of reverence—even, on occasion, a kind of love. And what better way was there to come to know such a place than to range freely across its seemingly limitless expanse in pursuit of game?

Once, while goose hunting, Charlie and I followed a wide V of honking Canadians over thirty or forty miles of snow-covered plains, only to see them descend upon a frozen swale thousands of yards beyond our reach. Leaving the Blazer in the driveway of an abandoned farmhouse, we crawled on our bellies across the whole of that frozen expanse, only to have the geese take to the air against a backdrop of yawning blue long before we got close enough to shoot. I remember lying perfectly still on my back in the snow, listening and watching as the birds made their escape, regretting none of it. In a way, that memory is the most vivid one I have of all my hunting days.

Shortly after dawn on the morning of April 16, 1867, while in the field against a mixed force of Cheyenne Dog Soldiers and Oglala Sioux in western Kansas, General Custer spotted a herd of antelope grazing in the distance a few miles from where the men of his command were preparing for the day's march. The sight of these creatures, reputed to be the fleetest on the plains, stirred something in Custer. Gathering his dogs about him, and ordering his bugler to follow, he took off in hot pursuit.

Abandoning himself to the chase, Custer followed the dogs until it became clear that they would never catch up to the fleeing antelope. However, no sooner had the general called the hounds off than he spotted a large, dark animal grazing a mile away. It was a buffalo bull—the first Custer had ever encountered. "Here was my opportunity," the general writes in *My Life on the Plains* (1874). "A ravine near by would enable me to approach unseen until almost in pistol range of my game."

Hunting buffalo with a pistol was a common strategy in those years. Although dangerous, it was considered more "sporting" than simply picking the poor brutes off with a high-powered rifle. The idea was to ride close enough to the buffalo to get a clean shot, yet not so close that the guts of your horse were opened in the process. As he tells it, Custer followed this plan to a T, but when the time came to pull the trigger, he balked. "Repeatedly could I have placed the muzzle against the shaggy body of the huge beast, by whose side I fairly yelled with wild excitement and delight, yet each time would I withdraw the weapon, as if to prolong the enjoyment of the race."

Finally, however, the buffalo began to flag, and Custer knew the moment of truth had arrived. He rode up to the buffalo's side, raised his pistol, and was about to squeeze off a shot when the animal wheeled suddenly and threw out a horn. The horse he was riding veered sharply to the left, and to keep from falling, Custer grabbed at his reins with both hands. "Unfortunately, as I did so," he writes, "my finger in the excitement of the occasion, pressed the trigger, discharged the pistol, and sent the fatal ball into the very brain of the noble animal I rode."

The horse, a favorite of his wife's named Custis Lee, folded up like a cheap umbrella, and Custer flew over its head to land in a heap on the prairie. "Here I was," he concludes, "alone in the heart of Indian country, with warlike Indians known to be in the vicinity. I was not familiar with the country. How far I had traveled, or in what direction from the column, I was at a loss to know. In the excitement of the chase, I had lost all reckoning."

Soon the men of the Seventh Cavalry came to their commander's rescue, and Custer began enthusing on the merits of buffalo hunting as a sort of cross-training for cavalrymen and their mounts. "I know of no better drill for perfecting men in the use of firearms on horseback," he would later write, apparently without irony, "than buffalo hunting over a moderately rough country."

I lay with my back to the north bank of the Arkansas, J. C. Higgins in hand, waiting for Charlie to give the signal for us to spring into action. On the other side of the embankment, out of our line of sight, a tom turkey announced his arrival with a high-pitched gobble that got louder with every step he took in our direction.

Now? I asked Charlie with my eyes.

No, he shook his head. *Not yet.*

It was the spring of 1981. I was seventeen years old. Although I had been hunting for five years and had shot everything from mourning doves to Canadian geese, I had never hunted wild turkeys before, and I was more than a little anxious to get my bird. Charlie had bagged his on the opening day of the season, more than a week before, but so far all of my attempts had been marred by my seemingly innate inability to sit still. "Your average turkey has got a pathetic vocabulary," Charlie's brother

Bob had explained over and over, "but he can spot the head of a match from a hundred yards away. What do you suppose all your fidgeting looks like to him?"

To get around the problem, Charlie and I devised a plan whereby we would call my turkey in from behind the natural blind of the riverbank. I could fidget all I wanted to, and the only thing the turkey would see would be the sexy plastic decoys we had set out in the clover for his enticement.

And so there I lay, dressed from head to toe in camouflage, while Charlie gave a series of low clucks on his wooden box call. A deep-voiced tom answered immediately, his gobble so close now I broke into a sweat hearing it.

Now? I pleaded again.

No, Charlie shook his head.

Waiting like this was pure torture to me. Like Custer, I preferred headlong action, and to hell with the consequences. And so when Mr. Tom, himself impatient, let loose with his loudest gobble yet, I didn't even bother to look at Charlie but rather sprang forth like some oversized jack-in-the-box. Coming over the top of the embankment, I caught sight of the turkey in the flowering alfalfa, his tail feathers completely fanned, strutting wildly before the plastic decoys. Never in my life had I seen anything so beautiful—and at the same time so absurd.

However, no sooner had I noted this strange dichotomy than I began a long, gravel-crunching slide down the embankment. Alarmed by the noise I was making, the turkey stopped in mid-strut and swung his head around to look at me. Our eyes met briefly, and then the toe of my boot caught on something, and I pitched forward into the air. Clutching my gun against my belly, I went into a deep tuck, tumbling end over end before slamming headfirst into the mud at the edge of the alfalfa.

Jumping to my feet, I saw two things simultaneously. The first was the turkey flapping his black wings in retreat, and the second was Charlie standing beside me, his auto loader raised in anticipation. I raised my gun, too, and we both fired at the same time. I saw a blast of orange and felt a gritty backwash hit me between the eyes. Instantly I dropped my gun and brought my hands to my face. My ears rang painfully, and my eyes felt as if someone had tossed a bucket of dirt into them.

"Are you all right?" Charlie asked. Only to me it sounded more like *Arrrrgggggg yyoooouuuuallllllllllriiiiiiiiiigggggghttttt?*

I shook my head and blinked.

"Yyoooouuuuugggoooooootttttyyoooouuurrrrbiiiiiirrddd!" he said, holding the dead turkey by its long, skinny neck.

"Wwuuunnnnddeeeerrrrrfuuuuulll," I heard myself say.

Later, picking up the discarded gun, I saw that its barrel had been splintered to pieces. It was like something out of a violent cartoon, the aftermath of Bugs Bunny plugging the end of Porky the Pig's gun with a carrot (only in my case, the carrot was mud). However, in spite of the persistent ringing in my ears and the gunpowder embedded in both of my cheeks and the fact that even then I suspected Charlie had really shot that bird, when the time came, later that day, I still held its body aloft in triumph so that my mother could snap a photograph of us.

Custer would pose for many such photographs during his five years in Kansas. Indeed, by 1869, when the Kansas Pacific reached the Colorado line, Custer's name as a hunter rivaled and in some quarters eclipsed his reputation as a military man. In his camp on Big Creek near Fort Hays, Custer and his wife entertained a constant stream of visitors from the East—titans of industry, the idle rich—most of whom came to Kansas with one goal in mind: to ride alongside the general and his pack of hounds in the headlong pursuit of buffalo and antelope. The most famous of these guests was Grand Duke Alexis of Russia. Young, handsome, and impossibly rich, the duke arrived on the central plains in January 1872 during a much-publicized tour of the United States. The highlight of the tour was to be a buffalo hunt organized by General Philip

Sheridan and guided by the likes of Custer and Buffalo Bill Cody. Accounts of the affair make it clear that no expense was spared in making sure the twenty-two year-old duke had the time of his life.

By direct order of Sheridan, the first kill of the hunt was to be reserved for the duke. However, this turned out to be easier said than done. Excited and unaccustomed to shooting from a running horse, the young duke emptied pistol after pistol without so much as grazing a buffalo. Finally Buffalo Bill lent the duke his favorite rifle and horse, whipped the animal to within ten feet of a flagging bull, and held him there. Firing at point-blank range, the duke dropped the buffalo in its tracks, at which point a great cheer went up, champagne was brought forward with the wagons, and a series of elaborate toasts was made.

To the Grand Duke! Hurrah!

However, this was not the end of the fun.

Chalkley Beeson, who later operated the Long Branch Saloon in Dodge, served as guide for the Colorado leg of the hunt. Left behind with General Sheridan and the supply wagons so that the duke could use his horse, Beeson soon found himself in the direct path of one of Custer's famous charges. "The bullets were dropping all around us," Beeson remembers, "and we *infantry* made tracks down the hill trying to get out of range." Sheridan, too short in the leg to run away, threw himself on the ground while the bullets whistled overhead. But later, after the smoke finally cleared, Sheridan, known throughout the army for his profanity, lit into the entire party, Custer and the duke included. "I don't know what kind of language Pa Romanoff used to Alexis when he got mad," Beeson would later remark, "but that slip of royalty got a cursing from Phil Sheridan that day that I bet he will never forget."

In spite of these mishaps, the grand duke always considered the days he spent hunting with General Custer and Buffalo Bill to be the highlight of an otherwise boring and officious life. When the duke died in 1908, he still owned the mounted buffalo heads and other trophies he had carried away from his tour of the plains. As for Custer, the hunt marked the end of his Kansas interlude and the beginning of a more nakedly ambitious period that would culminate in his death at the Battle of the Little Bighorn in 1876. By then, of course, the numberless herds of bison that once covered the high plains had been pushed to the very brink of extinction.

In the fall of my senior year of high school, an optometrist from Little Rock approached my father about leasing the hunting rights to a farm my family owned northwest of Dodge City. The man—I'll call him Bud—was in the habit of bringing clients up from Arkansas each November to hunt on the opening weekend of pheasant season, and he was always looking for ways to reduce the hit-and-miss quality of the enterprise. "I just want to make sure the boys have a good time and get a lot of birds," he said to my father in his thick, Southern drawl. "That's why I'd like to buy exclusive rights to hunt your ground."

My father, who did not hunt himself and couldn't understand why anyone would, turned down this offer out of hand. However, a moment later, he pointed to me and said, "But if you're bound and determined to pay someone to hunt, why not hire him? He's starting college next year, and I know he could use the money."

"Well, how about it?" Bud asked. "You wanna make some money?"

"Sure," I said, although in truth I was far from certain. "Why not?"

So began my brief career as a professional hunting guide.

Not content to saddle myself with the chore, I soon brought in Charlie as my partner. This wasn't hard to do given the amount of money Bud was offering: a hundred dollars a day for each of us, plus a five-dollar bonus for every bird bagged. With ten guns in Bud's party and a bag limit of four birds per gun, a good day of hunting promised to net each of us something on the order of two hundred dollars, and that was before tips, which Bud promised would be generous. "These Arkansas boys like to have fun," he said. "And they don't mind paying for the privilege."

Eyeing these potential profits greedily, Charlie and I set to work planning a weekend of hunting such as Bud and his boys would never have experienced before. We had every detail of the weekend worked out, from where we would start a day's hunting, to when and where we would stop for lunch, to the prizes we would award for "Best Shot of the Day," and so on. In short, we tried to give them the kind of experience we would have enjoyed, failing to see that our ideas about hunting and those held by Bud and his boys were completely at odds.

They shot at hens as well as roosters, quit looking for downed birds after only a minute or two, and carried flasks of peppermint schnapps or Wild Turkey into the field with them. The drinking began with ceremonial shots at sunrise, gained steam over lunch at a local watering hole, and remained alarmingly steady after that. By three in the afternoon, half the party was so drunk they retreated to the comforts of Bud's rented Winnebago to sleep it off. The other half, meanwhile, continued to hunt regardless of whether they could walk straight or hold a gun steady. Hunting might have represented something sacred to Charlie and me, but to Bud and his boys it was a chance to get drunk and blow off some steam away from the pressures of their careers and family lives. Bud made this clear enough when Charlie and I complained to him about the drinking and all of the other breaches of the hunting code. "I ain't paying you boys to give us a *sermon*," he said, laughing. "Your job is to lead us to where the birds are, remember?" At this Charlie and I exchanged wide-eyed glances. We both knew we should have quit right then and there, but for some reason we couldn't bring ourselves to do it. For my part, I felt as if I had signed some kind of contract or holy pact, and now I had to see it through no matter what happened.

It was late in the afternoon of the second day, and we were hunting a field of my father's just west of Dodge City. Charlie and I and a group of five or six of Bud's boys had just walked our last swath through the field, pheasants retreating before us, and now we had them trapped at the far end, where Bud and several of more his boys stood blocking the birds' escape. It was the old surround tactic, and we had performed the maneuver beautifully. All that remained was to be patient and to take the birds one at a time as they took to the air between us.

One after another, the pheasants broke cover, Bud and his boys sending volley after volley into the sky after them. Meanwhile, Charlie and I kept our guns on safety, hoping that Bud or a couple of the more sober boys would get lucky and bring down a bird or two. There were several high passing shots in a row, all misses. Then a low-breaking bird got up directly between me and a hunter perhaps forty yards from me. The man, who had stumbled from Bud's Winnebago only minutes before, raised his gun unsteadily and pointed it directly at me. I closed my eyes tightly and turned away. A half second later, I heard the blast of his gun and felt a stream of pellets slap against my shoulder, back, and neck.

"Jesus Christ!" I yelled, my hand seeking out a burning spot on my neck. "The son of a bitch just shot me!"

A horrified silence followed, as the other hunters in the field shouldered their guns one by one, and Charlie and Bud hurried over to where I stood fingering the wound on my neck. As for the man who shot me, he just stood there with a confused expression on his face. "Who shot him?" I heard him ask the guy next to him. "What in the hell's going on?"

"Good thing you looked away when you did," Bud said nervously, as Charlie dug out the single pellet that had broken skin. "You could've had an eye put out easy. Well, how about it? You okay?"

I remember looking into the man's beady, bloodshot eyes and wondering how it was I had agreed to any of this. In later years, revisiting this moment in places as far-flung as Kairouan, Tunisia, and Buffalo, New York, I would characterize it, sometimes in a comic mood and sometimes not, as my Last Stand.

"You can keep your goddamn money, I don't care," I said, ejecting the unspent shells from my gun and leaving them on the ground at Bud's feet. "As for me, I'm done. I'm through with this whole messed-up deal."

And with that, I walked straight out of that field and into the rest of my life.

Sisyphus of the Plains

> The gods had condemned Sisyphus to
> ceaselessly rolling a rock to the top of a
> mountain, whence the stone would fall
> back of its own weight.
>
> —Albert Camus

Every summer between the ages of twelve and seventeen, I worked for my father on the farm he bought in his early forties as part of a larger, midlife upheaval I had no way of understanding at the time. Buying the Knoeber place was a return of sorts for my father, who grew up on a farm and still had farming in his blood despite the decade he'd spent managing an auto body salvage yard in town. But for the rest of our large family, particularly those of us who followed the old man out to the Knoeber place to work, the change was more like a violent revolution, complete with purges and summary executions and forced marches into a bleak countryside.

Before my father bought the Knoeber place, my life consisted of a pleasantly bland round of activities centered on the parish school I attended and the scrappy, working-class neighborhood where my parents overbuilt when they moved to town in 1967. There were birthday parties and baseball games and Scout meetings to attend, the building of tree houses and underground forts, swimming at the American Legion pool on hot summer days, picking cherries in the Bagbys' backyard, and riding my banana-seat Schwinn to the DQ to get a Peanut Buster Parfait. As for my father, his existence was little more than a rumor. Holidays and periods of home improvement aside, he was rarely home. He attended Mass with us on Sunday morn-ings, and sometimes, if certain elements of the universe came into miraculous alignment, we would picnic in Wright Park or pull a boat to Cedar Bluff Reservoir, a couple of hours away. But mostly he worked, and unless I happened to go to work with him, his world and mine rarely overlapped.

Then, in the mid-1970s, he sold the parts business to buy Knoeber's, and although we continued to live in town (my mother had tasted country living once before in their marriage and refused to go back), just about everything else about our lives changed dramatically. The days of ignorant bliss came to a close, and I came to see our life for what it was: an absurdist drama in-volving ceaseless toil and the witnessing of titanic struggles with fate in which my father played the part of tragic hero.

I vividly recall the first day I went to work for my father. It was a frigid March morning in my fifth-grade year at Sacred Heart Cathedral, and the entire school was abuzz with the news that a massive winter storm was expected to dump several feet of snow on the southern plains. All that remained for the storm to be classified a blizzard was for the wind to begin its char-acteristic howl, and that began a little after ten o'clock that morning. At twelve thirty, I returned from the school cafeteria to find my father standing outside the door of my classroom in his coveralls and galoshes. His straight black hair was flecked with snow, and the corners of his brown eyes were shot with blood. I remember wondering how it was he had managed to find my classroom, and I was embarrassed to see the mess the snow from his galoshes was making on the carpeted hallway.

"Dad, what are you doing here?" I asked.

"Get your coat," he said.

"But what about school?" I asked. "Does Mom know you're here?"

"Get it and come on," he repeated, before starting back down the long, narrow hallway.

I was still standing there, immobilized by shock, when my teacher, a stern old nun named Sister Urban, came up from the cafeteria. "My dad was just here," I reported breathlessly. "He said to get my coat and go with him."

"Well," Sister Urban said. "What are you waiting for? Get your coat."

This came as an even greater surprise than the snow or my father's sudden apparition in that place he had never been known to appear before. It was as if the entire adult world had conspired to astound me. Even so, I ran to get my coat.

"The cattle are out," the old man informed me as I climbed into the cab of his pickup. "You'd better put on some of those clothes." On the floorboard of the truck was a pile of overcoats and galoshes he'd raided from the hall closet of our house in town. I remember thinking, *He knows where Mom keeps the clothes?* The thought that my father had chosen me to help him in this time of crisis vibrated somewhere deep within me, and as I pulled on coveralls and overshoes, I imagined the two of us bringing the cattle to safety accompanied by a melodramatic soundtrack straight out of some 1960s TV Western—*Bonanza,* say, or better yet, *The Big Valley.*

But first I must be taught to drive. This my father accomplished right there in the snow-filled parking lot, as my classmates and Sister Urban looked on from the second-story windows of our mission-style school. The pickup was an old International with a three-speed stick. "Ease your foot off the clutch and feed her a little gas," he said. "If you need to stop, just throw her into neutral. It's not hard."

"What about other cars?" I asked.

"There aren't any other cars where we're going," he answered ominously.

I was nervous, anxious to do a good job, perhaps to win the old man's praise, but the truth was he barely paid attention. When I stalled the truck at a stop sign, as happened several times, or took a corner a little too wide, all he said was, "You're all right" or "Just keep on doing like you're doing."

Otherwise he continued to gaze out the window at the accumulating snow.

The cattle were spread out across two counties, and getting them back to where they belonged was an arduous task involving much in the way of human and animal suffering. My part was to guide a truck loaded with alfalfa between snow-filled ditches (hence the impromptu driving lesson), while my father and several of my brothers and cousins prodded the exhausted cattle from behind. It was terrible, grinding work. A hired cowboy who helped out that day got frostbit across the tips of his fingers. For years afterward, whenever I ran into this ghostly, rail-thin man, he'd wave the fingers in my face and say in his nicotine voice, "There's the little shit who sat on the heater in the feed truck while the rest of us froze our asses off!"

But I have other memories of the blizzard. Ice forming in the moustaches of the horsemen. Yearling cattle dead on the side of the road, their black hooves sticking out of the drifts like tombstones. How unnaturally white the sky was, the sun little more than a dull yellow globe. The way the wind swept across the frozen surface of the earth like some malignant force . . . I hadn't known the world was capable of such power. I thought snow was for sledding or the building of backyard igloos. But now I had witnessed another side of things, and I carried the knowledge with me like a doom. When I returned to Sacred Heart a few days later, it felt as if a couple of years had gone by. At the door to my classroom, I looked into Sister Urban's pale blue eyes and saw for the first time that she, too, possessed the terrible knowledge.

"Well, young man," she said. "Did you learn anything helping your father?"

I had indeed, but I didn't trust myself to put any of it into words. Instead, I mumbled something about snowdrifts and electric fences and stole past her into the warm classroom, happy to be among the uninitiated once again.

That summer, I started working for my father in earnest. This was no tag-along, pretend job. We left for work before eight in the morning and didn't return home until long after dark—sometimes as late as ten thirty or eleven o'clock at night, at which point we would scarf down a warmed-over dinner, stand in the shower for ten minutes, and then fall into bed. Half an hour later, or so it seemed, my father would shake me awake—"Get up, it's time"—and the cycle would repeat itself. We worked six and sometimes seven days a week. During one stretch, with more at stake than I could comprehend, we worked something like forty-five or fifty days without taking so much as an evening off. Gradually I lost track not only of what day or week it was but also what month. June? July? August, maybe? I remember asking my brother Joe if he knew, but he just shook his head at the question. "Who cares?" he asked rhetorically.

The Knoeber place was five hundred acres of black dirt with a dilapidated farmhouse and outbuildings that looked ready to fall in on themselves if the wind blew too hard. Three wells on the property supplied water to forty acres of flood ground and a couple of ancient center-pivot irrigation systems. At the time we took on the burden of these outdated sprinklers, they had not produced a crop in several years, and at least one neighboring farmer predicted they never would. "Those old water-drive systems are junk, more trouble than they're worth," the neighbor said. "You'd be better off selling them for scrap right now and buying yourself an electric system with a proper shutoff."

People were constantly giving my father advice like this. He should buy better equipment, plant better seed, use a computer program to track the fertility of his cows, and so on. To my knowledge, he never took any of it to heart. He was too independent and stubborn for that. He had his own ideas about how to do things and didn't care what other people thought or said about him. In reply to the neighbor who dared to call his sprinklers junk, he simply smiled and said, "Well, you're probably right about that. But we'll give them a try all the same."

Early that summer, as a sort of experiment or prayer, we planted a thick crop of corn in both circles. The problem with growing corn in a place like Kansas is the severe lack of rain. For the crop to survive, it must be irrigated around the clock for the entire three-month growing season. Even in the rare event of a downpour, the sprinklers keep right on going, pumping seven or eight hundred gallons of water a minute. In the parlance of irrigating, this is called "letting the sprinklers catch up."

However, the sprinklers on the Knoeber place never did catch up. In truth, they hardly ran at all. They had two basic modes: either they shut themselves down when they should have been running, or else they continued to pump water when they should have shut themselves down. We would spend ten or twelve hours slaving to get the well motor, the towers, or the shutoff system working properly. Finally, come nightfall, all of the problems would appear to be solved. Water would be coursing through the pipe, the towers would be creeping across the land at their designated intervals. We would sit together in the pickup, our headlights shining on the end tower, praying that our luck would hold. "By God, I think we've got her," my father would mutter. "I think she's gonna run this time."

And so we'd tramp home, exhausted as usual.

All too often, however, a terrible reality would await us the next morning. While we slept, one of the towers would get out of line, and the system would halt in its tracks. If we were especially unlucky, the mechanical water shutoff would fail, too, and the sprinklers would go right on pumping water at the usual rate of eight hundred gallons a minute. This was called "pumping in place." Even a few hours in this state meant towers so mired in mud that a couple of tractors and a winch truck would be required to pull them out. Meanwhile, in an irony only the Fates could have arranged, the rest of the crop would be burning up for *lack* of water.

During the years I worked for him, my father faced a crisis of this size and scope at least once or twice a month. Drought, hail, lightning, and tornados; fire and flood; insect plagues; equipment failure; catastrophic drops in the market price of wheat, cattle, or corn . . . If it wasn't one thing, it was another—and all too often, it was more than one thing.

One day the irrigation motor on the south sprinkler blew a head gasket. We threw a chain around it and used the bucket on the John Deere to haul the motor to the shop for rebuilding. But the chain broke halfway there, and the motor fell, and the tractor ran over it, snapping a front axle. And what did we find, when we went to fix the axle, but that thieves had broken into the pickup's toolbox and stolen the four-way tire tool.

"Let me see if I've got this straight," my brother Steve joked in his sarcastic way. "We have to replace the *four-way* so we can fix the *tractor* so we can rebuild the freaking *motor* so the freaking *corn* won't burn up?"

"You forgot the chain," my brother Joe added after a pause. "We have to fix that, too."

And so we did.

And yet not once, faced with these absurdities, did I ever hear my father curse or see him lose his temper. Believe me, there were plenty of times when I wished he'd have done just that—for my sake, if not for his own. *Is he really just gonna stand there and take it?* I'd wonder. His stoicism frightened me because it smacked of submission, and what boy wants to see his father submit?

Years later, reading Camus' *The Myth of Sisyphus* in a philosophy course at the University of Kansas, I had no trouble recognizing my father. The image of him pushing a massive boulder to the top of a mountain, only to see it roll to the bottom once again, was so apt I couldn't believe it hadn't occurred to me independently of Camus or the Greeks.

Harder to fathom was the belief Camus expresses at the end of his essay, where he writes of the "happiness" and "silent joy" Sisyphus finds each time he returns to the bottom of the mountain to retrieve his boulder. "The struggle itself toward the heights is enough to fill a man's heart," Camus writes. "One must imagine Sisyphus happy."

But how, I wondered, could anyone find happiness in such torture? To know from the outset that failure of one sort or another will be the result of one's labor, and yet still to find solace—joy, even—in the work itself? Such an idea flew in the face of the heightened (and largely erroneous) sense of justice I still harbored in those years.

Honestly, I don't think my father slept more than a couple of hours a night during all those summers I worked for him. One night, God only knows what time it was or what day of the week, I woke from a bad dream and wandered into the kitchen to get a glass of water. There he sat in his pajamas and work boots, eating a bowl of chocolate chip ice cream. The boots, I noted at a glance, were muddy and flecked with torn corn leaves. Obviously he had gotten up in the night and driven the eight miles to Knoeber's to check the sprinklers.

"Don't tell me," I said. "One of the water drives is down, right?"

"I got them shut down," he answered, taking a bite of the ice cream. "We'll deal with it in the morning."

"*Them?*" I asked with my usual outrage. "*Both* sprinklers were stuck?"

"Go on back to bed," he said. "It'll be a long day tomorrow."

A long day! I thought, shaking my head. *What the hell else was new?*

However, the Fates were not through toying with us just yet. Later that summer, driving out to Knoeber's one Sunday to check on the sprinklers, we found to our horror that one of them had twisted itself into a giant pretzel. Seven hundred gallons of water a minute shot geyser-like from the broken pipe. It was almost beautiful, in a grotesque sort of way. Looking up at the sight from our place in the road, we saw rainbows. Rainbows! *Isn't that a little much?* I wondered. *What's next? Being swallowed by a whale?*

"Well, I guess you'd better go shut her down," my father said, before beginning a slow, head-down walk into the field to inspect the damage.

By the time I was fifteen years old, I stood six feet tall and weighed 160 pounds. I could operate a tractor or combine, back a trailer using only the side mirrors, move a herd of cattle on horseback. I knew how to stretch a fence, mix and pour concrete, raise a wall, and shingle a roof. I could weld, solder, rivet, and screw. I was steady and dependable, had great stamina, and for the most part I did not complain, even on those days when one disaster followed another and bitching about it—or even quitting outright—might have been the only sensible response. Though still young, I was already "good help," as my father liked to say.

However, there had never been any question of my going into farming, not that I had ever expressed such a desire. My father had always been crystal clear about that. Farming and ranching was his dream. His sons would have to go out into the world and find dreams of our own to pursue. I can remember quite clearly the way it happened for me.

It was the summer between my sophomore and junior year in high school, and my job on the weeks-long wheat harvest was to take loaded trucks to the grain elevator at Howell, Kansas, a ten-mile round trip from Knoeber's. Between loads, perhaps four or five hours a day all told, I sat in the truck and read whatever was on hand, which in the first few days of the harvest consisted of a couple of trashy Harold Robbins novels. After consuming these in short order, I began smuggling books from my mother's library at home. With the hours my father worked, she'd had ample opportunity to read, and the shelves of her library groaned with handsomely bound classics, books like *Tess of the D'Urbervilles* and *Huckleberry Finn* and *The Count of Monte Cristo,* which she had bought as part of a subscription to this or that book club. Although I'd never been much of a reader up to that point, I soon found myself addicted, lost amid the gilt-edged pages to which I shamelessly added my fingerprints. In the space of a few short weeks, I devoured novels and story collections by an eclectic group of writers including Dickens, de Maupassant, and Dostoyevsky. What worlds! Paris in the nineteenth century. Czarist Russia. The moors of England. The island prison of Château d'If . . . All from the cab of a wheat truck parked on the edge of a dusty field in far western Kansas.

Harvest over, I carried my newfound addiction with me into the cab of my four-wheel-drive John Deere, pulling the tractor over for fifteen minutes of every hour to continue whatever book I was reading at the time. When the fifteen minutes were up—and how fast they went!—I put the book aside and reluctantly resumed my plowing. For the next forty-five minutes, the characters continued to live within me. Often I would find myself inventing entirely new story lines or plot twists to keep the characters—and myself—busy. Thus did Tess escape the censure of Victorian England and Huck and Jim float past New Orleans to discover new lives in South America. Looking back on all this now, I see that these freewheeling imaginings of mine were in fact my first attempts to write fiction. In the absence of anything better to do, I was opening a space in my mind and allowing it to fill. I was fashioning a text that, however flawed, was meant to stand in for—even replace—the world I actually lived in. This, too, was part of my education on the Knoeber place. Indeed, by the time I finished work that summer, I had come to believe that one day I would seek my own adventures in the world—adventures that would serve as a sort of prelude to writing about them.

And so it happened.

In 1984, I left Dodge City and traveled east to attend college, moving from there to graduate study abroad in England and my first teaching post at a Faculty of Letters in North Africa. After returning to America, I completed a doctorate in English, then enrolled in the fiction writing program at Washington University in St. Louis. I was thirty years old and newly married, brimming with confidence and enthusiasm about writing. In my third semester in the program, I bought a used typewriter at a garage sale in University City and dedicated myself to a strict schedule of a thousand typed words a day. In a little under three months of sustained effort, I completed a first draft of an autobiographical novel set in Tunisia. The book, appropriately titled *Fools Rush In,* was rough-hewn and flawed in ways too fundamental to ignore. However, it existed, and that fact alone inspired and thrilled me.

After reading this rough draft through to the end, a famous visiting writer asked in a good-natured way how long I thought it would take to produce a workable revision.

"I don't know," I said. "Another three months, maybe?"

The writer, who would go on to achieve even greater fame for a beautiful and strange story set amid a sheep camp in Wyoming, just looked at me and grinned. Had I known the meaning of that grin, I might have saved myself a lot of heartache and self-torture in the months and years to come. But then again, maybe not. Maybe we all have to learn these lessons in our way. In any case, five years and four tedious drafts later, the book still refused to be finished.

I accomplished other things in those years, of course. I married and started a family, published a well-received book of literary criticism, taught hundreds of undergraduates and graduate students, and so on. Yet to me all of this paled in comparison to the frustration and failure I'd experienced trying to finish my Tunisia novel. How could someone work so hard toward such a singular goal, devoting literally thousands of hours—evenings, weekends, entire summers off from teaching—only to see it all come to nothing in the end? Where was the justice in that? How could the gods who survey our puny lives from above allow such a thing to happen? These were questions to which I knew there to be no good answers even as I tortured myself by asking them.

About the time I was throwing in the towel on my ill-fated first novel, my father was supervising the lifting of a two-ton wheat box onto a naked truck frame when the box slipped from the forks of the front-end loader and landed on him, crushing his right leg. By the time the hired man who'd been operating the loader reached my father's side, the old man was on the verge of losing consciousness. "Get it off me, then call 911," he managed to say. The hired man did as he was told, and a couple of hours later, my father underwent the first in what would eventually be three separate surgeries.

He was past seventy and in poor health, suffering from arthritis, stomach ulcers, and chronic anemia, to name only a few of his many ailments and injuries, most of them directly related to the relentless pace and towering pressure that had characterized his life for so long. However, none of this challenged my father in quite the same way the accident involving the wheat box did. Shortly after the first surgery, in which a steel rod was run through the middle of his broken femur, x-rays revealed that his right hip was broken as well, and a second surgery would be required to replace the first rod with a longer one. This second surgery was complicated and risky, and it did not go well. When the rod was pulled out, the femur broke into a dozen pieces and the gruesome patch-up job that followed was itself thoroughly botched, leaving the orthopedic surgeon who performed the procedure visibly shaken afterward.

During the long rehab that followed, my brothers and I talked often on the telephone about whether the old man would ever walk again, let alone return to work.

"He will, don't worry," my brother Dave predicted.

"How can you be so sure?" I asked. "One leg longer than the other, the grinding pain, all that bone growth in the hip . . ." Just talking about it made me shudder.

"You know what he said to me the other day?" Dave asked after a brief pause. "He said, 'If I'm not back to work in six months, shoot me.' That's how I know. That's how determined the old son of a bitch is."

As it happened, my father beat even his own prediction, returning to work on the ranch after only four months of driving our mother crazy with his presence in her living room. However,

the next couple of years were a torture. Unable to take painkill-
ers on account of his stomach problems, he endured terrifying
levels of chronic pain and could not sleep more than an hour
or two unless his body was propped up in a La-Z-Boy. Hesi-
tantly at first, and then with greater conviction, he began to
talk about undergoing a third operation—this one in Kansas
City or Wichita instead of Dodge City.

"Why is he putting himself through it?" I asked more than
once. "Why doesn't he just call it a career and retire, like a normal human being would do?"

"I keep telling you," Dave answered. "If he can't work, he
wants to be shot. That's it. That's his whole outlook on life."

As luck would have it, my father's third surgery took
place over Christmas break, so my wife and kids and I were
able to visit him in the rehab hospital in Wichita where he spent
a month undergoing physical and occupational therapy. From
talking to my mother on the phone, I knew that the surgery
had been a partial success at best. The hip and joint issues had
been replaced by a persistent foot drop, the result of nerve damage sustained during the long operation. Still, despite the bad
news about his foot, my father was in remarkably high spirits,
making daily progress in physical therapy and even beginning
to show signs of the old tenacity and grit.

"How are you feeling?" I asked.

"Good," he said. "There's a bucket under the bed full of
all the hardware they took out of me. Have a look." I glanced
at this bucket, and it was indeed full of pulleys and brackets
and other grotesqueries. "How about you?" he then asked.
"How's work?"

The question took me by surprise. Although we had logged
many hours together on the farm and later the ranch, we had
never really talked about me or my dreams. This was my fault as
much as it was his. From a boy, I'd been taught to be independent, to keep my own counsel and avoid complaint whenever
possible, and gradually all of that solidified into habit. Even
now, with nothing but time before us and a clear invitation to

talk, my first instinct was to brush the question aside. "Oh, it's going all right," I said.

"Well, good," he said, quickly changing the subject to the upcoming Super Bowl.

Later, though, on the drive home to Indianapolis, I found myself returning to my father's question. However, each time I tried to approach it, the only thing that popped into my brain was that bucket of gruesome hardware under my father's hospital bed. That's how badly the son of a bitch wanted to return to the job that had almost killed him. That's how much he wanted and needed to work. *To work:* nothing more, nothing less. It wasn't about fame or money or more abstract forms of success. No, it was just about the doing of it, the not giving up, the daily satisfaction of working hard at something for the simple reason that you yourself had chosen to do it, the small but steady joy in that.

What was it that Camus had written about Sisyphus? "The struggle itself toward the heights is enough to fill a man's heart. One must imagine Sisyphus happy."

According to a non-Homeric tradition, Sisyphus was the father not only of Glaucus, whose body was torn apart by horses during the funeral games of King Pelias, but also of Odysseus, the hero known for the ten eventful years it took him to return from the Trojan Wars. As for me, I'm still on that journey, still learning from and fleeing the example of my father, still setting out daily on that long, torturous trip back home.

A Most Romantic Spot

Like all Indian encampments, the ground
chosen was a most romantic spot. . . .

—George Armstrong Custer,
My Life on the Plains (1874)

August 2005. Just past dawn on a clear, crisp morning, I
leave my parents' ranch on Sawlog Creek and head west across
the plains toward Colorado. Later the air will turn hot, but for
now I leave the windows on my Jeep Cherokee rolled down so I
can feel the wind in my face and smell the alfalfa drying in the
bottom ground lining the Arkansas River. The day before, I had
stood in my driveway in Indianapolis, trying to explain to my
eight-year-old daughter that I was off to visit a couple of Indian
villages I had been reading about.

"What kind of Indians?" Ria asked.

"Southern Cheyennes."

"And are they expecting you?"

"Well, not exactly," I said, explaining that the places I had
in mind to visit were not actual villages but rather sites where
villages had once stood, and then only briefly, more than 140
years ago.

Ria nodded doubtfully. "Will you take some pictures, so I
can see too?"

"Of course I will," I said, bending to kiss her goodbye.

I did not add that these places, each less than a half day's
drive from where I grew up, were the sites of Indian massacres.
Why? Because she was too young to understand? Because I
was too lazy and pressed for time? Maybe. But then again, the

massacres themselves cannot account for my desire to visit the ground in question. For despite all the reading I've done, much of it in dry tomes of military history, I have no particular interest in lines of attack or defense, lists of the dead and wounded, or even warring accounts of what "really happened." Instead, I just want to stand where the events themselves took place. I want to see what the Indians saw in those places. I want, if possible, to imagine them there, in that landscape I have known my whole life. Because as much as I hate to admit it, part of me does not quite believe that there ever were Indians in Kansas. After all, it's not as though the Southern Cheyennes or Kiowas or any of the other Plains tribes have left actual ruins behind. They were no-mads. As the novelist Thomas McGuane once quipped, it would take a shovel to know they had been there at all.

The plains I travel across this morning rise steadily toward the foothills of the Rocky Mountains, five hundred miles to the west. Where the land is open and flat, it is generally plowed up to grow wheat or, with the aid of irrigation, milo or corn. Only the hilly, gulch-ridden land along bluffs and creeks has been left in grass. And yet it is this ground, deemed marginal by the standards of modern agriculture, that always draws my eye on trips back home. To my way of thinking, that's where all of the beauty and mystery of the place resides. The rest is still Kansas; it just isn't my Kansas.

Stopping for breakfast at a gas station in Syracuse, six-teen miles east of the Colorado line, I am greeted by an eight-foot-high mural of a mountain man sitting his horse next to a buckskin-clad Indian princess rather improbably holding a lamb in her arms. Across the street, adorning the side of a Ford dealership, is a larger mural of a wagon train pushing west under an armed escort. Murals of this sort are a com-mon sight in small western towns like the one where I grew up. Though marred by inaccuracies and a creeping sentimentality, they express a pride in place that is hard-won and true.

An hour after leaving Syracuse, I roll into Lamar, Colorado, population 9,000, where a twenty-foot-high statue, "Madonna of the Trail," rises up in the parking lot of the old Santa Fe depot. The statue, erected by the Daughters of the American Revolution in the late 1920s, depicts a muscular, sun-bonneted woman striding confidently across the plains with an infant in one arm and a rifle in the other. As I stand taking a picture of the massive statue, an eastbound freight begins a slow crawl past the depot, reminding me that my business is not here but forty miles to the north, along the south bend of Big Sandy.

To anyone even vaguely familiar with western history, Sand Creek stands out as a blight and a scar. It was there, on November 29, 1864, that Colonel John M. Chivington, a Methodist minister turned Indian fighter and would-be politician, led a group of 700 mostly untrained volunteers in a dawn attack on a peaceful Cheyenne village. Following repeated assurances of peace, most of the village's warriors were away hunting buffalo. Both an American flag and a white flag flew above the village that morning; seeing this, two of Chivington's officers refused the order to attack. Others, however, did not, and somewhere between 130 and 160 Indians, most of them women and children, were killed when the volunteers rained cannon fire down upon them. When the fighting ceased, around two o'clock in the afternoon, Chivington's men proceeded to scalp the dead and hack their bodies to pieces. Fingers, ears, noses, both male and female genitalia—all these were cut away from the dead along with their scalps, the whole bloody mess later put on display before a theater in Denver. Although the massacre caused an outcry in the East, in the paranoid West of those years it was largely met with applause, and the men responsible for it went largely unpunished. In 1887, a railroad town a few miles south of the massacre site was christened Chivington, Colorado, in dubious honor of the man known on the frontier as "The Fighting Parson."

Today, the area where the massacre took place is rolling rangeland covered in sparse grass and sagebrush. As in western Kansas, the landscape is treeless except for a few cottonwoods lining the riverbeds and creeks. The Southern Cheyennes began calling this place home around 1820, when, along with their friends the Arapahos, they drifted south from the Platte in search of horses. White traders following the trail to Santa Fe began showing up not long after this, and by the early 1860s, trade along the route had expanded to the point at which a military post, Fort Lyon, was established to protect it. Fort Lyon was where Colonel Chivington and his men launched their infamous attack.

Turning right on Colorado Highway 96, I begin a slow crawl through the town of Chivington. Most of the dozen or so buildings still standing in the town are vacant or in the process of falling in on themselves, the lone exception a Quaker church bearing the name *Friends of Chivington*. As I consider the manifold ironies of the name, the right rear tire on the Jeep blows out, and I wobble to a stop by the roadside. In the twenty minutes it takes me to change the tire, not a single car or truck passes by. It's just me and the prairie dogs and the wind and heat. Then, as I am tightening the last lugs on the spare, a mud-spattered ranch pickup appears on the horizon, and moments later, its fifty-something driver rolls to a stop beside me.

"Need any help?" the rancher asks without getting out of his truck.

"Thanks," I say. "I think I've got it."

"Your tag says Indiana," the man observes. "What is that, eight hundred miles from here?'

"More like a thousand."

At this, the man whistles and removes his feed cap, revealing a white forehead. Next he asks me what I am doing that far from home, and when I tell him, he whistles again and puts the cap back on. "Sand Creek, huh? Are you an Indian?"

"Me?" I ask incredulously. "Not even close."

"Well then, I wouldn't expect a grand welcome up there or anything like that."

"No? Why is that?"

"Go on up there. You'll see." And with that, he tips his cap and continues on his way.

It is an innocent enough conversation, yet it puts me on edge all the same. In his subtle way, the man has made me feel like an interloper, a complete outsider. But while it is true that I haven't planned the trip particularly well, relying almost entirely on a six-year-old Rand McNally that shows the site to be at the end of a long, dead-end road, it is also true that very little separates this landscape from the one in which I spent the first twenty years of my life, and part of me feels that it is nothing short of my birthright to follow that road to its end and see whatever there is to see there.

I turn off the highway onto a sand road made slippery by recent rain. Eight miles later, the road comes to the dead end depicted on my map. Only it isn't really a dead end, I see now, but rather a T. From here I can plainly see a line of cottonwoods snaking down from the northwest. I turn right and keep going. The land stretches away for miles, nothing but sagebrush and sand hills with a few head of cattle grazing here and there. Then, a mile past the dead end, I come to a ranch road that is heavily gated and locked, with not one but two NO TRESPASSING signs adorning it.

So here's that grand welcome, I think, getting out of the Jeep to stand before the locked gate. There's no question that the rutted lane on the other side of the gate is the road to Sand Creek. Perhaps a mile beyond the gate, the land rises into a series of high bluffs I recognize from pictures of the massacre site. When leaving Kansas that morning, I imagined myself standing atop these very bluffs looking down into the creek below, which I knew to be wide and dry and lined with tall cottonwoods. All I have to do now to make that dream come true is to climb over a steel gate and begin walking; ten minutes later, I'll be there.

And yet I hesitate, unable to take a single step. Why? The act of trespassing on remote, privately owned rangeland is a common occurrence in the West, and it's not as if I'm here to steal or vandalize. Still, I can't bring myself to do it. Somehow I just don't feel justified or welcome. After all, none of *my* people died or were wounded here. Literally, I have no ground whatsoever to stand on.

And so, rather than climbing over that gate, as part of me still wants to do, I settle for snapping half a dozen pictures. *It serves you right,* I pause to write in my notebook. *Did you really think it would be that easy? That you'd just walk in there and have all your questions answered?* Shaking my head ruefully, I cast a final look at those bluffs, make a brief promise to myself, and head back down the road to Kansas.

Next morning, I start south from the ranch on Highway 283, headed for the Washita Battlefield National Historic Site near Cheyenne, Oklahoma. There, on a frigid morning in November 1868, almost exactly four years to the day after the massacre at Sand Creek, General George Armstrong Custer led the Seventh Cavalry in a dawn attack on the sleeping village of the Cheyenne chief Black Kettle, whose small band had borne the brunt of the attack at Sand Creek as well.

Has there ever been an Indian more gullible and unlucky than Black Kettle? Each time he appears in the histories, he's in the middle of some improbable speech about how his people have nothing to fear from the white man. Yet no sooner is the speech delivered than a bugle blares in the distance and the aforementioned white man arrives amid a barrage of rifle and cannon fire. So it was at Sand Creek, where Black Kettle famously raised a large American flag over his lodge (a flag he had been given at a peace council in 1860), only to see those of his people who sought shelter beneath the flag slaughtered before his eyes. And so it was at Washita, too. Only on this occasion, neither Black Kettle nor his wife Medicine Woman Later (who was shot nine times at Sand Creek) managed to escape.

In *My Life on the Plains,* Custer paints a heroic picture of the Seventh Cavalry battling through deep snow to achieve what the general terms "a great and important success over the hostile tribes." Insofar as they remember it at all, contemporary Americans know a very different version: that supplied by Thomas Berger in his 1964 novel *Little Big Man,* wherein Jack Crabb and his Cheyenne grandfather, Old Lodge Skins, walk unharmed through the whole of Custer's army even as bullets rain down all around them. "Pay no attention to them, my son," Old Lodge Skins tells Jack. "I have now seen that it is not our day to die."

Of these two accounts, Custer's is by far the more graphic and thorough, supplying such details as how the army surrounded the village and systematically destroyed all of the Indians' belongings, including more than eight hundred horses and their entire winter supply of food and clothing. However, it is Berger's mock-heroic account that we recall. Why? Because there is some kind of release in comedy we cannot hope to find in gore? Because the truth about what happened in certain places in the West has a tendency to make those places uninhabitable for us in an imaginative sense?

I don't pretend to have answers to these questions. All I really know as I wend my way south is that I feel myself spurred on by a single, ludicrously simple desire, and that is to stand at the original site of Black Kettle's village, maybe take a snapshot or two to show my daughter when I get back home. If I can do that, so I tell myself, then maybe my failure at Sand Creek will no longer stick in my throat the way it does now.

And so I pass through Laverne, Oklahoma, Home of Jane Jayroe, Miss America 1967. And Beautiful Shattuck, Home of the Shattuck Indians, where the neon sign above Tom's Quick Stop features a smiling, cartoon Indian in a loincloth and eagle feathers. Eight miles farther south, the famed Antelope Hills rise suddenly into view, and suddenly I understand how it was that Custer's scouts regarded these hills as a beacon of sorts, certain to lead them to where the Indians were camped. I lean forward in my seat, anticipating. I cross the Canadian River and keep on going.

With the trip meter on the Jeep reading 160 miles, I enter the town of Cheyenne, Oklahoma, population 778. Grain elevators rise on the right side of the road. On the left, just off the main square, is a sign for the Black Kettle Museum. While waiting for a hamburger in a crowded café, I skim a recent issue of the *Cheyenne Star*, learning, among other things, that a local boy has raised a ten-pound cabbage and the Miss Harvest Queen 2005 pageant is scheduled for September 10. Despite my Wranglers and Tony Lamas, the waitress who brings my lunch immediately pegs me as an outsider. When I ask how she can tell, she nods at my notebook and camera and says in a high, laughing voice, "Most folks who come in here have got the place pretty well memorized by now."

The valley I've come to see is located two miles west of Cheyenne, on State Highway 47A, just below an impressive range of red rock bluffs. Managed by the United States Park Service since 1996, the Washita site includes a concrete overlook, interpretive plaques, and a winding, mile-long, self-guided tour. Beyond these few embellishments, however, the valley looks pretty much the same as it would have in the 1860s. When I pull up, a massive RV with the words GOD LOVE YA stenciled on the back stands idling in the parking lot. The vehicle's owners, a stout couple in their sixties, soon labor up the hill.

"How was it?" I ask.

The woman, wiping sweat from her brow, shakes her head and disappears into the RV.

"Oh, definitely worth the visit," her husband adds, smiling weakly.

When my fellow tourists are gone, I walk down a hillside of rock and scorched weeds until I come to a broad meadow in a horseshoe of the river. The place is an oasis of sorts, protected from the wind by the bluffs, with plenty of water, wood, and grass nearby. In a land filled with beautiful places, it might not draw a second glance, but here, on the open high plains, it registers as a kind of paradise.

Closing my eyes, I can hear the steady murmur of the river, which is really more like a small creek, and feel the rustle of the wind as it moves through the knee-high grass. Other details accumulate. A cow bawls for its calf in a nearby pasture. Grasshoppers collide in the grass at my feet. A horsefly lands on my left ear, takes a couple of steps, then buzzes away. When I open my eyes again, I can almost see the outline of the village, the tall white lodges opening to the east and arranged in kinship circles within the river's bend. Terrible things happened here. Black Kettle, shot from his horse, died and was scalped by Custer's Osage scouts within a hundred yards of where I stand. Yet for some reason I do not smell the odor of death or listen for the sound of gunfire. Instead, I imagine the place at peace. Why? What kind of renegade desire does that express?

I spend the next hour roaming the valley's three hundred acres, then drive to the Black Kettle Museum in Cheyenne, where I fall into a conversation about Custer with the woman ringing up my purchases in the gift shop. "Are you a fan of General Custer's?" the woman asks.

"Not really."

"Then why all the books?" she asks, nodding at the stack she continues to ring up.

I tell her I'm from Kansas and that Custer spent some time there in the years before the Little Bighorn.

"Kansas, huh? Then I suppose you've been to Pawnee Fork?"

I admit I haven't, and she pulls a book from my stack of purchases and opens it to a map of the Hancock Campaign of 1867. "There," she says, pointing a finger at a spot on the Pawnee Fork of the Arkansas River, halfway between Fort Larned and Fort Dodge. "I don't know if the Park Service has opened the site yet, but it might be worth your time to take a look."

I stand there laughing and shaking my head.

"What's so funny?" the woman asks, somewhat taken aback.

"Nothing," I say. "It's just that I've driven over seven hundred miles the last two days, and the spot you're pointing to is maybe forty miles from where I grew up."

"Well, there you go," the woman says, shutting the book with a thud.

It was the spring of 1867, a year and a half before Washita, and the United States Army was taking a beating in its war with the Indians of the northern and southern plains. The previous winter, Red Cloud's Sioux had succeeded in running the army out of Wyoming Territory, and rumor had it that the Kiowa chief Satanta had boasted he would achieve the same result in Kansas that spring. To forestall the expected attack, a large show of force, some fourteen hundred men all told, was mustered at Fort Leavenworth and sent west under the command of General Winfield Hancock—like Custer, a hero of the Civil War with no previous experience fighting Indians. A sizable press corps and not a few celebrities, Wild Bill Hickok among them, accompanied the expedition, the feeling being that wherever Hancock and Custer went, action was sure to break out in one form or another.

In fact, the expedition was a disaster from the first. Snowmelt and heavy rain turned the plains into a quagmire. Supply wagons sank to their axles in mud, and proper drilling of the troops, many of them raw recruits, was next to impossible. By the time Hancock's army reached Fort Larned in western Kansas, it was already April, too late for a winter campaign (not that one could have been mounted, in any case, without supplies). Then, on the ninth of April, a freak storm dropped eight inches of fresh snow on the plains. During the bitterly cold night that followed, Custer's troopers were ordered to keep their horses moving along the picket lines to prevent them from freezing to death.

Despite these conditions, an impatient Hancock sent word to a mixed group of Sioux and Cheyennes encamped on Pawnee Fork, some forty miles to the west, demanding that their head men come to the fort immediately so that peace talks could commence. When the chiefs arrived, exhausted, several days later, Hancock subjected them to a stern harangue. "The Great Father has heard that some Indians have taken white men and women captives," Hancock said. "He has heard, also, that a great many Indians are trying to get up war. That is the reason I came down here. I intend not only to visit you here, but my troops will remain among you, to see that the peace of the plains is preserved. I am going to visit you in your camps."

To this, Tall Bull of the Cheyennes replied that the Indians on Pawnee Fork were peaceful and that the real issue was white settlement, which was causing game on the southern plains to diminish fast. Soon there would be no buffalo at all, he complained. As for Hancock's threat to visit his village, Tall Bull warned, "If you go, I shall have no more to say to you there than here. I have said all I want to say . . ."

"I am going, however, to your camp tomorrow," Hancock repeated stubbornly.

What happened next goes a long way toward explaining why the army later became so enamored of dawn attacks on quiet, sleeping villages. While the Indians, fearing another Sand Creek, were forced to evacuate their village with few belongings and on winter-weakened ponies to boot, they still easily outmarched Custer and the Seventh Cavalry. For three long days, Custer continued the pursuit, yet in all that time, not a single Indian was seen, let alone captured or engaged in battle. It was, Custer would remark later, as if all fifteen hundred of the savages—men, women, and children—had vanished into thin air.

Angry at the failure and pointing to several killings the Indians were said to have committed while in flight, Hancock ordered that the entire village be burned to the ground. Before the first match was struck, however, a young reporter named Henry M. Stanley, who would later gain fame by tracking down the Scottish explorer David Livingstone in Africa, took a precise inventory of items the Indians left behind.

> 251 lodges, 942 buffalo robes, 436 horn saddles, 435 travesties [travoises], 287 bead mats, 191 axes, 190 kettles, 77 frying-pans, 50 tin cups, 30 whetstones, 212 sacks of paint, 98 water kegs, 7 ovens, 41 grubbing horns, 28 coffee mills, 144 lariat ropes, 129 chairs, 303

parflecks [parfleches], 5 curry combs, 67 coffee pots, 46 hoes, 81 flicking irons, 149 horn spoons, 27 crow bars, 73 brass kettles, 17 hammers, 8 stewpans, 15 drawing knives, 25 spades, 4 scythes, 8 files, 19 bridles, 8 pitchforks, 15 tea kettles, 90 spoons, 15 knives, 10 pickaxes, 1 sword, 1 bayonet, 1 U.S. mail bag, 74 stone mallets, 1 lance, 33 wooden spoons, 251 doormats, 48 rawhide ropes, and 22 meat stones.

The contents of this list ought to be required reading for anyone imagining that life in a Cheyenne village was some kind of idyll. Clearly a lot of work, much of it dirty and backbreaking (and performed by women) was required to keep fifteen hundred people from freezing or starving to death on the open plains. But from afar, if not up close, the village on Pawnee Fork struck both Stanley and Custer as a place of surpassing beauty. "The savages," Stanley wrote, "roaming at large over the whole country, can select, of a thousand and one lovely spots which Nature has so bountifully provided, the loveliest of all." Writing several years later, Custer echoed the sentiment. "Like all Indian encampments, the ground chosen was a most romantic spot, and at the same time fulfilled in every respect the requirements of a good camping ground; wood, water, and grass were abundant."

Romantic or not, it all went up in flames. "The dry poles of the wigwams caught fire like tinder," Stanley wrote for his audience back east. "Flakes of fire were borne on the breeze to different parts of the prairie, setting the prairie grass on fire. With lightning speed the fire rolled on, and consumed an immense area of grass. . . . Every green thing, and every dead thing that reared its head above the earth, was consumed."

On the day I set out to find the village, I head north from Sawlog Creek on Highway 283. Halfway to Ness City, I run into the dry Pawnee and begin following its south bank eastward toward the town of Larned, figuring that when I see the place I will be sure to know it. Four hours later, having zigzagged without success over mile upon mile of narrow, sand roads, I admit my mistake and drive thirty miles out of my way to ask directions from the rangers at the Fort Larned National Historical Site.

"Pawnee Fork?" the ranger manning the front desk asks suspiciously. "Why do you want to go to Pawnee Fork?"

"I just want to see it," I say with a shrug.

"You're not an artifact hunter, are you?"

"No," I say. "I'm a writer."

"A writer. And you want to . . ."

"Just look at the place. Maybe take a few pictures." As if to prove this last point, I hold up my five-dollar disposable camera in its yellow cardboard cover.

At this, the ranger sighs and takes a pen from the breast pocket of his uniform. While he draws a map of the village on the back of a postcard, I ask who owns the property. "We do," he says, handing me the makeshift map. "Just so we're clear— no smoking, digging, or camping out. Got it?"

Half an hour later, I pull up alongside a spot that would be indistinguishable from any other in the area were it not for a small limestone marker nearly hidden in the roadside weeds. INDIAN VILLAGE ON PAWNEE FORK, EARL GADBERY PRESERVE, the marker reads.

The place looks dry and unpromising. Earlier in the day, I drove by it at least twice without so much as slowing down. On one side of the marker is a plot of dusty wheat stubble; on the other a typical southwestern Kansas pasture showing signs of overgrazing. A half mile in the distance, however, a series of two-legged phone poles I recognize from the ranger's map rise up from the tree-lined creek. My pulse quickening, I backtrack a quarter of a mile to an unsanded field road and drive in a little deeper.

From here I see the first of a group of islands in the stream I've read about and seen represented in nineteenth-century maps of the village. After crawling over a four-wire fence, I descend into the dry creek bed, emerging moments later in a broad meadow surrounded on all sides by cottonwoods. *I'm here,* I think, the words of Custer and Stanley echoing in my brain. *A most romantic spot. . . . The loveliest of all. . . .*

As I stand there in the clearing, a sense of déjà vu begins to take hold of me. As was the case at Sand Creek and Washita, there is that same tucked-away, horseshoe feel of the place, that same mix of scenic beauty, protection from the wind, and easy access to water, wood, and grass. Seeing this third example of what the Cheyennes prized in a winter camping ground, I begin to understand, slowly at first, and then with a gathering speed and clarity, that these aren't the only such sites I know about or have visited in my life. Indeed, such sites are everywhere on the southern plains. As a child, I camped or picnicked in a dozen meadows more or less identical to this one. The chosen spot always looked like this, always felt special and safe, a world away from the unprotected monotony of the high plains. Invariably, people visiting the place for the first time would say, "Can you believe this is Kansas? I can't." My family's ranch on the Sawlog, which I count among my favorite places in the world, contains half a dozen such spots—each of them, I realize with sudden force, inhabited by ghosts.

Standing there, squinting my eyes in the harsh Kansas sun, I can almost make out the white circles of lodges dotting the prairie.

The Search for Quivira

It is not a hilly country, but one with
mesas, plains, and charming rivers with
fine waters, and it pleased me, indeed.

—Juan Jamarillo's *Narrative of Quivira*

I first became aware of the Coronado expedition in the middle of third grade, when my teacher, a young nun named Sister Fidel Marie, took our class on a tour of the stained glass windows in Dodge City's Sacred Heart Cathedral. Most of the saints depicted in the windows—Frances Cabrini, Martin de Porres, Rose of Lima—were New World saints of a fairly recent vintage, Sister informed us. However, only one of them had walked the very ground where we now stood.

"Which one?" we demanded to know.

"Father Padilla," Sister said, pointing to a blue window in the southwest corner of the church depicting a gaunt, gray-skinned monk with sad, wounded eyes. As we stood looking up at the window, Sister explained that Fray Padilla, good Franciscan that he was, had walked all the way from Mexico to what would become Dodge City, and that once he got to Kansas, he refused to leave. "Father Padilla was a missionary and a very holy man," Sister concluded. "He loved God and Kansas—even to the point of *dying* for them."

This last part struck me as unreliable nunspeak, and I remember thinking at the time, *She's got to be kidding. Who gives up his life for a place like this?*

But even so, I was intrigued. The idea that my flat, wind-blown home state had some connection to a period of time I associated with castles and knights in shining armor filled me with hope and longing.

Several years after this, as part of an obligatory course in Kansas history, I dutifully learned the most salient facts about the expedition, such as when it began and ended (1540–42) and the most probable route the conquistadors had taken through Kansas (due north from the Oklahoma border to Dodge City, and from there, up the Arkansas River valley as far as Salina or Junction City). However, bored teenager that I was, little about any of this impressed me. Only much later, after I had moved away from Kansas and begun to suffer the first twinges of nostalgia, did I begin to read books about the expedition, such as Castaneda's *Narrative* and Bolton's *Coronado: Knight of Pueblos and Plains*. What I discovered in these books shocked and thrilled me. The Kansas I had known all my life, defined by dilapidated Main Streets and blowing dirt, was nowhere to be seen; in its place was a hauntingly beautiful world of tall grass and sweetly flowing rivers that went by the mysterious name of Quivira.

Six miles east of Dodge City, all but lost amid an industrial corridor of beef-packing plants and feedlots, a thirty-eight-foot concrete cross rises from the low hills lining the north bank of the Arkansas River. Seen from below and against a backdrop of yawning blue, the cross, known locally as the Coronado Cross, looks curiously like a sword thrust into the hillside by an angry giant: either that or the headstone of some massive, anonymous tomb.

It's still dark when I pull my mile-worn Jeep into the scrappy roadside park beneath Coronado Cross. Just behind me, on US Highway 400, semis scream past carrying live cattle to slaughter, boxed and frozen beef in the opposite direction. In the final minutes before dawn, I train the Jeep's headlights on the park's six-foot-high roadside marker and begin reading.

The Coronado Historical Park commemorates Coronado's journey in 1540–41 searching for gold. Following the safe crossing of the treacherous Arkansas nearby, Coronado and his entourage celebrated a Mass of Thanksgiving in this vicinity.

The cross on the hill serves as a memorial of that first Christian service held west of the Mississippi on June 29, 1541.

What glory these words signify. If only they were true! In fact, the "Mass of Thanksgiving" featured so prominently here (to say nothing of the stories of Sister Fidel Marie) is mentioned nowhere in the firsthand accounts of the expedition I've been reading, and the idea that this Mass was somehow the first of its kind held west of the Mississippi is fanciful at best, and at worst an outright lie. After all, the expedition's entire route from Mexico to Kansas lay "west of the Mississippi," and the Spaniards of that era were known to celebrate Mass at the drop of a hat—far more often than they bathed or changed clothes. However, none of this irks me to the extent that the marker's brief mention of the "treacherous Arkansas" does. As anyone familiar with southwestern Kansas will tell you, the stretch of the Arkansas that runs through Dodge City has been dry for more than thirty years, its once "treacherous" waters drained by upstream irrigation and the building of Colorado's John Martin Reservoir. Indeed, to cross the Arkansas these days is to encounter no greater obstacle than derelict barbed wire and ankle-deep sand.

Is this what I've come here for? I wonder. *To have my dream of Quivira derailed by faulty signage?*

But even as I think this dismal thought, I know it can't be so. Quivira is out there somewhere, just waiting to be discovered. Hence the plan I have cobbled together with the aid of guidebooks and roadmaps: following in the footsteps of Don Francisco Vasquez de Coronado, I will cut a path across Kansas from southwest to northeast, searching everywhere along the way for signs of Quivira, that mythic landscape which from the first whispered rumors of its existence owned a dual reputation as both a paradise and a graveyard for the dreams of men.

The man we know as Coronado arrived in the New World in 1535, drawn across the ocean by the legend of the Seven Cities of Antilia. According to this curious legend, the Seven Cities were founded by seven Portuguese bishops who fled the Iberian peninsula in 714, shortly after the Moorish invasion. For centuries thereafter, so the legend went, the descendants of these bishops lived in splendid isolation, building a wealthy island paradise somewhere off the coast of Portugal. After Christopher Columbus's discovery of the New World in 1492, the search for the Seven Cities shifted across the Atlantic to the West Indies, Mexico, and eventually as far north as the Great Plains.

The Coronado expedition, a massive undertaking attracting a hodgepodge of mercenaries, landless nobility, and other gold-rush types, was one of the last and biggest of Spanish attempts to loot riches where there weren't any. For a year and a half, the expedition toiled ever northward, visiting hostile Pueblo lands in what later became Arizona and New Mexico before traversing the staked plains of Texas and, with a much reduced force, continuing north and east into the very heart of what is now Kansas. Along the way, the Spaniards suffered great hardships, spilled much Indian blood, and saw many wondrous things, including the Grand Canyon and the limitless bison herds of the lower high plains. However, no matter where they went or what marvels they witnessed, the treasure they had come so far to loot stubbornly refused to materialize.

No gold was discovered at the Zuni city of Hawikuh.

None at Acoma.

None at Tiguex or Pecos Pueblo.

None still amid the level wastes of the staked plains.

And so in May of 1541, having failed to find the Seven Cities in any of these more likely places, Vasquez turned his sights northward, to a province on the plains his Indian guides called Quivira.

The author of Don Francisco Vasquez's dreams of Quivira was a tattooed Wichita from the plains of Kansas whom the Spaniards called "El Turco," on account of his supposed resemblance to an Ottoman Turk. A captive of the Indians at Pecos Pueblo, the Turk was on loan to the Spaniards as a guide to the Great Plains, a region Vasquez intended to explore fully as soon as the ice was off the Rio Grande. To hear the Turk tell of it, Quivira was a place of mighty rivers and powerful kings whose subjects paid tribute in finely woven fabrics and precious metals. The Lord of Quivira "took his siesta under a large tree from which hung numerous golden jingle bells," "the common table service of all was generally of wrought silver," and "the pitchers, dishes, and bowls were made of gold."

Oro, oro, *oro* . . . To the soldiers in Vasquez's bedraggled army, the word itself was like a bell ringing in a faraway tower, calling them and calling them. Evidently the Turk understood this well, for during the whole of the winter of 1540–41, as the army sat shivering beneath blankets stolen from their Indian "hosts," he would talk of little else. And when the soldiers, playing a game of sorts, tried to trick the Turk, showing him jewelry made of tin and asking if it were gold, the Turk, Castaneda tells us, simply "smelled [the tin] and said that it was not gold, that he knew gold and silver very well, and that he cared little for other metals." What a magnificent liar he was!

In the spring of 1541, newly installed as the army's chief guide, the Turk led Vasquez and his men out of their winter camps on the Rio Grande and onto plains so flat and devoid of landmarks that a sea compass had to be used to stay the course. Here disaster befell the expedition in myriad forms—hunger, thirst, and a "violent whirlwind," or tornado. Badly shaken by these setbacks, Francisco Vasquez finally sent the bulk of his army back to its camps on the Rio Grande, vowing to continue the search for Quivira with a smaller, more nimble detachment of thirty handpicked men.

Guided by a bit of magnetized iron hung from a silk thread, the party traveled north in a series of forced marches that in thirty days brought them to a ford in the Arkansas River long used by buffalo and traveling bands of Indians. Three days beyond the ford, somewhere between present-day Kinsley and Larned, Kansas, the Spaniards encountered their first Quivira, or Wichita, Indians, and here something extraordinary happened. "The general," Juan Jaramillo tells us in his brief chronicle, "wrote a letter to the governor of Harahey and Quivira, believing that he was a Christian from the shipwrecked fleets of Florida."

A Christian from the shipwrecked fleets of Florida?

Should we doubt that a glimmer of hope yet remained in the heart of Don Francisco Vasquez, here is our evidence to the contrary.

US Highway 56 follows the Arkansas northeast from Dodge City until the river makes a dramatic turn southward ninety miles later at the aptly named town of Great Bend. The road here roughly parallels the old Santa Fe Trail, passing by Fort Larned and Pawnee Rock State Historical Site, as well as Cheyenne Bottoms and Quivira National Wildlife Refuge, a pair of wetlands connected by a scenic byway. These attractions aside, however, the land is mostly flat and farmed up, the fields terraced to conserve rain or carved into massive circles watered by center-pivot irrigation systems. Here and there, a lonely oil well stabs at the ground like the needle of some giant sewing machine.

As I drive through this land I know so well, I try to imagine what it must have looked like to Vasquez and his men four hundred years ago. By all accounts, they saw it during a period of high rainfall, not the near-drought conditions I encounter. At that time, central Kansas was home to an estimated 150,000 Wichita Indians, a number nearly impossible to fathom (by 1874, a combination of war and disease had reduced the tribe to four bands totaling 671 individuals). Buffalo, antelope, deer, and elk were plentiful, to say nothing of bears, mountain lions, wolves, beavers, ducks, geese, turkeys, quail, prairie dogs, and thousands of other species of wildlife. As for the land, it was covered as far as the eye could see in a thick carpet of native grass through which wildfires swept with regularity, keeping trees and other obstructions to a minimum. Upon witnessing this part of Kansas for the first time in 1866, a young George Armstrong Custer felt moved to declare it "the fairest and richest portion of the national domain, blessed with a climate pure, bracing, and healthful." Today, of course, all that is a distant memory. Like every other section of the country, Kansas must earn its keep. How? By turning topsoil, groundwater, and liquid fertilizer into corn and wheat, grass and grain sorghum into beef. That is the reality of Kansas, the long-term destiny of the place

And so I motor through scrappy Great Bend with its towering grain elevators and faltering oil industry, continuing from there through the towns of Ellinwood and Chase, before crossing finally into Rice County, where a wooden billboard posted high above the roadway declares in capital letters, LYONS: LAND OF QUIVIRA.

Will this be it? I wonder, leaning forward in my seat.

The final leg to Quivira took the Spaniards through the lush middle valley of the Arkansas and Smoky Hill Rivers, a paradise of tall grass and bracing streams that was also the site of their greatest disappointment yet.

"After traveling seventy-seven days over these barren lands, our Lord willed that I should arrive in the province called Quivira, to which the guides had been leading me," Vasquez would write in a letter to the king of Spain dated October 20, 1541. "They had pictured it as having stone houses many stories high; not only are there none of stone, but, on the contrary, they are of straw, and the people are savage like all I have seen and passed up to this place. They have no blankets, nor cotton with which to make them. All they have is the tanned skins of the cattle they kill. . . . The natives there gave me a piece of copper that an Indian chief wore suspended from his neck. I am sending it to the viceroy of New Spain, for I have not seen any other metal in this region except this and some copper jingle bells which I am [also] forwarding to him."

The note of despair here is almost unbearable. Everything Vasquez had, was, and hoped to become had been riding on the gamble of Quivira, and here his final roll of the dice had come up snake eyes. There were no more dreams to follow, no more legends to explore—it had all been a wild goose chase, a terrible dead end. A scapegoat must be found to pay the price for this. The soldiers demanded it, their cries focused on the head of the Turk. Francisco Vasquez is said to have resisted their demands for as long as he could before turning the Indian over to be garrotted in the night, his body disposed of in secret to prevent an uprising among the Indians of Quivira. According to one chronicle, a meat cutter named Francisco Martin carried out the deed, twisting a rope around the Turk's neck until his eyes bulged and he died.

An hour northeast of Lyons, the land begins to ripple and rise. The fields are green with winter wheat, the pastures heavy with cattle. It's a little after eleven o'clock, more than three hours into the day's journey, and I'm headed for a butte called Coronado Heights, reputed to be the outermost spot in Kansas visited by Vasquez and his chosen thirty.

I come into sight of the butte, which rises three hundred feet above the valley floor, long before I reach it. At its base, a switchback road leads past a bullet-riddled entrance gate to a large stone tablet bearing the inscription CORONADO 1541. Farther up, a set of crumbling stone steps leads to the first of a series of picnic areas built directly into the hillside. At the east end of the butte, a two-story stone castle rises to stand sentinel over the valley below. Seeing this fake yet oddly impressive castle, I break into a fit of private laughter. *What's next?* I wonder. *Knights in shining armor?*

After parking the Jeep at the first of the picnic areas, I walk across the flat top of the butte, which stretches three hundred yards from end to end, and ascend the steps of the faux castle. Above a doorway on the second floor, a stone marker attributes the building of the castle to a Works Progress Administration project dating from the mid-1930s. On either side of the doorway, a stream of visitors have paused to carve their names into the soft brown stone. *Roy. Cristal. Dara. Tommy. Jesus Aldazvega 8/02.* After passing under the WPA marker, I emerge onto a balcony offering a view of the valley stretching eastward toward the Flint Hills, a patchwork of hay fields and bottom ground planted to wheat, milo, and corn. Perhaps a mile to the south, a combine is busy cutting a field of sorghum. Even at this distance, I can see the yellowish-orange grain as it flows from the long arm of the machine into the bed of a waiting semi. Witnessing this, I recall the words of a passage from Jamarillo's chronicle.

"This country has a fine appearance," the passage reads, "the like of which I have never seen anywhere in our Spain, in Italy, or part of France, nor indeed in other lands where I have traveled in the service of his Majesty. It is not a hilly country, but one with mesas, plains, and charming rivers with fine waters, and it pleased me, indeed. I am of the belief that it will be very productive for all sorts of commodities."

The passage, long a favorite of Kansas history teachers, always left me cold whenever I encountered it as a child. The Kansas I knew looked nothing at all like Jamarillo's description. And because I took the man's words at face value, completely missing the strong note of ambivalence in them, I failed also to see the extent to which disappointment as much as approval or awe inspired his chillingly accurate prophecy. Only now, thirty years later, do I make the connection, the two of us joined across the centuries by our separate disappointments. Unlike Jamarillo, however, who gazed into the future and imagined a Quivira tamed by the plow, I find myself looking in the opposite direction, longing for a glimpse of the place as it was when he saw it, before the production of cattle and corn turned its surface inside out.

It's a futile wish, I know, as silly in its way as expecting to find cities of gold on the vast, windswept prairies. But try as I might, I can't seem to shake it. The dream dies in one place, only to be born again farther down the road. *This isn't it, either,*

I hear myself mutter, my eyes traveling upward from the harvest scene to fall once more on the distant Flint Hills, the last place I'll visit in my search for Quivira.

O In the spring of 1542, as Vasquez and his men prepared for their long journey home, Fray Juan de Padilla electrified the expedition's winter camps by announcing that he would not be going with them as planned but instead would retrace his steps across the plains to take up a missionary's life among the Indians of Quivira. Upon hearing this dramatic declaration, sixty of Vasquez's soldiers immediately volunteered to accompany the priest, and only the intervention of Francisco Vasquez himself prevented a mutiny from taking place. In the end, only a small party consisting of Padilla, a Portuguese horseman named Andres de Campo, and two Indian lay brothers was authorized to make the journey.

Pushing a mixed herd of sheep and mules before them and traveling at most fifteen miles a day, the party forded the Arkansas River near Dodge City sometime in early July and arrived at the first Quiviran villages a week or so thereafter. By all accounts, Padilla received a warm welcome among the Wichitas. However, at some point, perhaps as early as a few weeks or months after his arrival in Quivira, the priest began to speak of visiting the tribe's eastern neighbors and longstanding rivals, the Gaus, or Kansa, Indians. Why Padilla made this fateful decision remains a mystery. According to one theory, advanced by the Spanish historian Moto Padilla, the priest's "heart burned within him, and it seemed to him that the number of souls of that village was but a small offering to God." However, this is but one view of the matter, and a highly biased one at that. A more radical theory, put forward in the 1960s by the Franciscan historian Fray Angelico Chavez, holds that Padilla had never intended to remain long among the Wichitas. "He had not crossed the great plains once more merely to return to the cross he had blessed, as the pious chroniclers relate," Chavez insists. "It was the Seven Cities of Antilia that beckoned like an ever-receding mirage."

Whatever accounts for the priest's decision, historians agree that in practical terms it amounted to little more than an act of suicide. At a day's journey from the Quiviran villages, hostile Indians caught up with Padilla and filled his body with arrows, after which they covered it, in the words of Moto Padillia, "with innumerable rocks." Campo and the two Indian brothers, meanwhile, somehow managed to return to Mexico, where, in the years that followed, the legend of Fray Padilla grew to include many fantastical elements, including reports of floods, fireballs in the sky, and a total eclipse of the sun on the day he is said to have died.

At least two spots in Kansas claim to be the final resting place of Fray Juan de Padilla. The most picturesque of these is a hill south of the Flint Hills town of Council Grove, and this is the one toward which I point the Jeep upon climbing down from the castle at Coronado Heights. By now it is early afternoon, and by my own calculations, I will not make it home to Indianapolis before midnight. Still I feel compelled to continue the search. Like Vasquez before me, the farther I progress, the more certain I become that I am *almost there*.

The Flint Hills are the last great swath of North American grass not surrendered to the plow. Because the soil here is thin and full of chert, farming never got a foothold. Alfalfa and the occasional plot of wheat is grown in the lowlands, but on the treeless, higher ground, grass still reigns supreme. Early each spring, the pastures are burned to clear the way for new growth, and by late April hundreds of thousands of head of cattle have been shipped in for an intensive grazing season that lasts only three months out of the year. By late summer, the season is over and the cattle have been shipped away, leaving the hills as empty as they were before the trucks arrived. It is in this state of seemingly preternatural emptiness I find them as I wend my way eastward from Gypsum to Hope to Council Grove.

In Council Grove, a town of two thousand people founded by a grandson of Daniel Boone, I waste half an hour trying to find the Padilla monument before wising up enough to ask directions at the Kaw Mission Historical Site, where the woman in charge, who is in the process of closing up, allows me into the mission library long enough to photocopy a map from an old guidebook.

"Are you Catholic?" the woman asks as we wait for the photocopier to warm up.

"Yes," I say. "But that's not why I'm here."

"No?"

"I'm looking for Quivira."

"Quivira, huh?" she asks, handing me the photocopied map. "Isn't that a lake up by Kansas City?"

"I'm looking for the actual place," I say, "the *real thing.*"

The woman looks at me like I'm crazy, which in a way I guess I am.

Ten minutes later, I stand on a high, windswept hill, looking at a ten-foot cairn of native rock and mortar that rises pyramid-like from the surrounding plains. In the center of this curious monument, which dates from the earliest days of the Great Depression, a bullet-dented brass plaque bears the following inscription:

THIS MONUMENT MARKS THE PLACE
OF THE MARTYRDOM AND DEATH
OF
FATHER JUAN PADILLA
FIRST FRANCISCAN MISSIONARY
TO KANSAS
DEC. 25, 1542

It goes without saying that the central claims made by the authors of this plaque are false. After all, who can say for sure where on the plains Padilla was killed, let alone on what date? By now, however, I have ceased to care about such matters. In fact, I spend no more than a minute or two snapping photos of the monument before turning away from it to take in the roll and sweep of the surrounding landscape.

Although it is November, far from the period of their peak beauty, and a string of power lines mars the view to the south, these hills are a sight to behold. "What is the grass?" Whitman asks in his most famous poem, answering the question in part, "I guess it must be the flag of my disposition, out of hopeful green stuff woven." My disposition is not nearly as hopeful as Whitman's, yet whenever I am in the Flint Hills, this line of his always comes to me. For despite the dusty road I drove in on, or the sight of those power lines strung like gaudy lamps across the southern horizon, or even the pile of rocks and mortar that is my ostensible purpose for being here, this spot yet remains a place where it is at least *possible* to imagine what the plains must have been like in that long-ago time before they were given over entirely to the production of "commodities."

Is that enough? I wonder. *Would you call that Quivira?*

The question lingers, stubbornly refusing to be answered, long after I climb back into my Jeep and leave the vast, still-undiscovered country of Quivira behind me.

PART III
OF HORSES, CATTLE, AND MEN

Horse Latitudes

A canter is a cure for every evil.

—Benjamin Disraeli

The worst month of my life was spent in an unaircondi-
tioned hotel room in Kairouan, Tunisia, in September 1989.
I had no friends and no money, an unfinished master's thesis
hanging over my head, and a case of dysentery so bad I might
have died had the hotel staff not forced me to drink cup after
cup of salted rice water. Throughout my weeks-long illness,
I could hear the sounds of horse-drawn carts echoing in the
cobblestone streets just beneath my window. *Clippity clop, clippity clop, clippity clop* . . . Sometimes, when a cart was parked
directly in front of the hotel, I could hear the horse itself snort
or shift in its traces. These sounds, so otherworldly and yet so
familiar, never failed to comfort me. Gradually the desire to get
well again got mixed up in my mind with the need to stroke the
withers of these animals, which I could hear but not see. *The
horses,* I would murmur in my delirium, *I've got to get down to
the horses* . . . Entire days were spent in this hallucinatory state.

When finally I recovered enough to leave the hotel, I de-
scended the stairs on wobbly legs and stood in the intense sun-
light of the Place des Martyrs, waiting for one of my phantom
horses to appear. At last one did, staggering to the curb before
a two-wheeled cart loaded with onions. The animal was little
more than skin and bones, its rump covered in open wounds
from where the driver, a boy of twelve or thirteen, had whacked
it repeatedly with a length of splintered wood. Ignoring the
driver's shouts to keep my distance, I stepped into the street and

rubbed the poor animal along its neck and ears, understanding for the first time how it was that Nietzsche was driven to insanity by the sight of a horse being beaten on a public street.

"*Les chevaux sont . . . la plus noble des créatures,*" I scolded the boy in halting French. "This one deserves far better treatment than he's getting from you."

"He's old," the boy replied, shrugging.

"If I give you money," I asked, "will you feed him a little grain tonight?"

"His teeth are very bad," the boy answered, holding out his hand. "But give me the money anyway, and I'll try."

Digging in my pocket, I came up with a five-dinar note, the last of the money I had changed after arriving in Tunis from London. "Here, take it," I said, "and remember . . ."

"*La plus noble, oui,*" the boy said. "I know, I know . . ."

Days to come, as my strength returned and I took on a demanding teaching schedule at a university in the suburbs, I made sure to bring a carrot or apple with me whenever I ventured into my old neighborhood near the Place des Martyrs. Before long all of the cart drivers knew me. "Here he comes!" they would shout. "*L'Anglais fou qui nourrit les chevaux!*"

They meant the name derisively, but that's not the way I took it. As far as I was concerned, those run-down horses they beat so mercilessly had all but saved my life.

Horses evolved on the plains of North America some 45 to 55 million years ago. Starting out as beagle-sized, multitoed creatures inhabiting a damp, primeval world, they changed along with their environment until they became the fleet, long-necked, single-toed animals we know today. By contrast, *Homo sapiens sapiens,* today's human beings, are relative Johnny-come-latelies, having emerged from the evolutionary record only about 50,000 years ago.

Around 9000 BC, horses spread from North America to Asia, to Europe, and finally to Africa. Not long after this, the land bridge across the Bering Strait disappeared under the melting ice pack, leaving the horses of North America isolated on a changing continent. Within a thousand years, they slipped into extinction along with the sloth and the mastodon, not to return until the Spanish brought them on ships in the early sixteenth century.

According to tradition, the first horses to return to the New World were the sixteen that Cortes unloaded at Vera Cruz in 1519, of which eight were said to be bay or sorrel, three were gray, two brown, one black, and two piebald or paint. More breeding stock arrived soon after, and by 1541, the conquistador Francisco Vasquez de Coronado had little trouble rounding up fifteen hundred horses for his expedition to what would later be New Mexico and Kansas.

The spread of horses across the plains proceeded rapidly after that. In 1719, the French explorer Du Tisne reported to his superiors in Louisiana that the Wichita Indians, who had never seen a horse before Coronado appeared among them in 1541, owned upwards of three hundred of the animals, which they "esteemed greatly" and with which they would not part for any price. A hundred years later, the American explorer Stephen H. Long put the number of horses owned by the Pawnees at somewhere between six thousand and eight thousand head, or roughly four horses for every warrior in the tribe.

The flyer said FREE RIDING LESSONS and featured a picture of a horse jumping a tall hedgerow. It was November 1986, and I was in my first semester as an exchange student at Essex University in Colchester, England. In those days, Colchester was a grim, wet garrison town ninety kilometers up the A12 from London. The place smelled of fried fish, unemployment ran into the double digits, and most nights the pubs were overrun with drunken soldiers, skinheads, and heroin-addicted punks. Needless to say, this was not the picture of England I'd had in mind when I left my home on the plains to seek adventure abroad.

The same day I spotted the flyer, I walked two miles in drizzling rain to meet the owner of the stable, an angular, middle-aged woman named Jane or Elizabeth (I forget which), whose tangled, gray-at-the-roots hair and filthy barn coat announced confidently to the world, "I am the sort of person who has ceased to give a damn about anything but horses."

"So you're a Yank," Jane observed, looking me up and down. "Ever mucked out a stable?"

I shook my head. "I've done farm work since I was a kid, though."

"Splendid," she said, showing me a mouthful of tobacco-stained teeth.

I spent the next hour shoveling horseshit into a wheel-barrow and hauling it up a muddy hill to a field behind the main barn. When I finished, Jane saddled one of the lesson horses, an ancient gray gelding, and led him into a large hilltop arena. There Jane's eyes narrowed, her manner stiffened visibly, and her voice took on an abrupt, almost angry quality. "No, no, no!" she barked when I stuck my muddy boot into the left stir-rup, preparing to mount. "That's not how we do it. We face the *back* of the horse. I thought you said you'd ridden before."

"I have," I said. "Western."

"Well, no wonder," Jane said.

Once she had shown me the proper way to mount a horse, Jane went on to demonstrate the correct method of sitting an English saddle. The whole thing felt stiff and pompous and was nothing like what I was used to—not that Jane cared about any of this. "We are not rounding up *dogies* on some Texan cattle station," she announced. "Neither are we preparing to *hurl* a lariat. We are *riding*. Do you understand?"

"Yes," I answered through gritted teeth.

At this, she hooked a longe line to the side of the horse's halter and stepped back twenty feet into the middle of the arena.

"What are you doing?" I asked.

"Preparing to longe the horse, of course."

"But I thought I was going to ride."

"You are, yes. But first we must do something about your dreadful posture. Now, *straighten* your back and get your *heels* in line with your *hips*. You're slouching!"

And so it went. Week after week, I mucked stables for free, and in return Jane did everything in her power to kill off any joy it was possible to feel while riding. She'd have made an excellent ballet or piano teacher. "Goodness, your hands!" she'd cry out as I rode in circles at the end of her long leash. "I have seven-year-olds who hold their hands more even than that! Heels down! Toes up!" Hearing this, I'd be seized by a desire to run her down where she stood in the middle of the arena. That accomplished, I'd jump the arena fence and be gone into the countryside beyond.

I did none of this, of course. Instead, I joined the campus saddle club, whose stock-in-trade was large trail rides deep into the neighboring moors. On one such ride, I witnessed something that reminded me what had drawn me to riding in the first place. We were stopped at a country crossroads and had been ordered to hold our horses so that a group of foxhunters could ride through at a trot. Here they came, one after the other, all of them posting leisurely in time with their horses. It was a pleasing sight, albeit nothing to write home about. Then, just as we were preparing to resume our own ride, a final member of their group, an older, jockey-like man with a white pencil mustache, came barreling past us at a dead run. Whereas all of the other riders had skirted the hedgerow that lined the road where we had stopped, the old man went right over it, his body rising in unison with the horse, so that the two of them, rider and horse, appeared not just to glide over the hedge but rather to *fly*.

That was twenty-five years ago, yet I still wake some mornings dreaming about it.

Horses are a precocial species, which is to say they are capable of standing and running within a short time after birth. Man is the opposite, an altricial species. Years after birth, he is still dependent on others to carry, feed, and protect him from harm.

Horses have the largest eyes of any land mammal, providing a range of vision greater than 350 degrees. Their ears rotate up to 180 degrees, allowing them to hear in all directions without having to move their heads. By contrast, man strains to see what is directly before him and is often fatally deaf to all sounds but those that please him.

Horses walk at four miles an hour, trot at eight miles an hour, and gallop at twenty-five to thirty miles an hour. They can sleep standing up or lying down and require only an hour or two of REM sleep every few days to meet their minimum requirements. Man, meanwhile, hesitates to walk a city block under his own power and requires fourteen to sixteen hours of REM sleep per week just to stave off idiocy.

Horses are prey animals, evolved over millions of years to survive by dint of attentiveness and flight. Man is a predator. Whenever a prey animal catches his attention, his deepest instinct is to hunt it down and eat it.

Given these differences, can the mysterious partnership that developed between horses and men over the centuries be viewed as anything other than a miracle?

In the years I was growing up there, the grasslands surrounding Dodge City, Kansas, were a regular mecca for horses, many of them worthless and rarely ridden. My cousin-in-law Kim Goodnight owned a couple of such animals on his and my cousin Beth's farmstead north of Dodge City. There, under Kim's tutelage, I had my first riding lesson, a five-minute affair that consisted of the transmission of three basic rules or ideas: (1) kick the horse to go, (2) pull back on the reins to stop, and (3) if you should happen to fall off, pick a soft place to land. "Think you can handle that?" Kim asked.

I nodded, full of a teenager's brash confidence.

"Good. Let's get you introduced to Jack."

Jack was a thirteen-year-old paint gelding that shared a five-acre pasture with another of Kim's horses, a fat grulla mare whose name I've forgotten. "You'll find that Jack's barn sour and a little mulish but otherwise bulletproof," Kim remarked as we saddled him up.

"Bulletproof?" I asked.

"Easy to catch, and he doesn't buck, bite, or kick. Those are traits you'll come to appreciate, if you keep riding."

"What about the mare?" I asked, nodding at Jack's pasture mate.

"Whole different ball game," Kim said, giving Jack's front cinch one last tug before climbing aboard his John Deere and disappearing into a nearby milo field.

I had been anticipating this moment for a while by then, and my expectations could not have been higher. I expected to ride hard and go fast, while at the same time maintaining a Zen-like balance and poise—all movements in sync, no separation at all between thought and action, no *effort* at all, just a transcendent, gliding motion, like an eagle soaring above a bottomless canyon.

Jack, however, had other ideas. No sooner did I climb into the saddle and try to ride away from the barn than he locked his legs at the knee and refused to budge. I moved my hips back and forth and prodded him in the ribs with the heels of my Converse All Stars. "Hey now!" I yelled. "Get going! Ha!" In response to this, Jack pivoted on his back feet and turned to face the barn, as if to say, "*That's* the only direction I intend on going."

So much for soaring like an eagle, I thought.

In the barn, I found a two-foot length of nylon rope with a hondo tied into the end of it. Applying this improvised whip to Jack's backside, I managed a painfully slow zigzag across the pasture. The trip lasted five minutes and took far more out of me than it did out of Jack. However, a reward of sorts awaited at the far end of the pasture, for no sooner did I turn Jack around to face the barn than he took off in a bone-jarring trot, holding the gait without further bidding until he fetched up before the barn door, where the fight to get him to go commenced all over again. In this herky-jerky way, like a sailboat tacking into a strong headwind, then turning to glide freely and with full sail, I managed to cross the pasture a dozen times in the space of an hour—not exactly a stellar showing, given all the work that was required of me to make it happen.

Even so, I was hooked. I loved Jack, loved the staccato feel of his movements beneath me, the way his feet hit the ground in such steady and reliable rhythm, four beats at a walk, two at a trot, three at lope (if you could get him to lope—not an easy proposition). I loved the way his ears moved to indicate where he was looking, the way he rolled on the ground like a big dog when the saddle was taken off, the sucking noises he made when drinking from the water trough. Young as I was, I felt that I was discovering all of this for the first time. No one before me, not the Plains Indians or the nomads who rode with Genghis Khan or even the knights of the fabled Round Table, had ever noticed or experienced any of these things. Two or three times a week, more often in the summer, I made the trek out to Kim and Beth's place to ride, at first limiting myself to the five-acre pasture but then venturing farther and farther afield.

Then Jack ate some bad grain, bloated like a hippo, and died. The news devastated me. Every time I saw a paint horse in a pasture somewhere my eyes would well up and I would cry. This period of mourning lasted a week, maybe two. Then I got on my Suzuki and rode back out to my cousin's place.

I saw the grulla mare standing in the far corner of the pasture as I turned into the gravel driveway. She lifted her blue head from where she was grazing and looked at me steadily, as though sizing me up. I knew from talking to Kim that riding this horse would be nothing at all like riding Jack. Whereas Jack was mulish but predictable, the mare was responsive and quick but also prone to sudden explosions of cantankerous ill temper. Even so, I figured I'd give riding her a shot. If nothing else, getting kicked or bit would give me something else to think about than Jack's sudden demise.

I caught the horse, snubbed her to a post, and threw a blanket and saddle on. Choosing a curbed bit with some stopping power should I need it, I led the mare into the pasture and climbed on. No sooner had my butt hit the saddle than the horse took off like a shot, slowing down only to throw in a buck every ten yards or so. Holding the reins in one hand, I gripped the saddle horn with the other and held on for dear life. From the corner of the pasture, I could hear Kim yelling, "Turn her! Put her in a circle, for Christ's sake!" I did as I was told, yet still the mare ran, nostrils dilated, hooves pounding the ground furiously. For more than twenty minutes she kept it up. After a while, I loosened my hand on the saddle horn; then I let go of it altogether. I stopped pulling back on the reins and let the mare have her head completely, concentrating instead on matching my rhythm with hers. By the time she ran down to a trot, and finally to a walk, I felt as if a switch of some sort had been thrown in my brain. *So this is what it means to ride,* I thought. *This is what it's supposed to feel like. . . .*

Later that same day, the mare would buck me off the back of the saddle and dropkick me halfway across the gravel lot in front of the barn, but not even that could dampen my growing enthusiasm.

Horses were first domesticated on the steppes of Eurasia sometime around 4000 BC. Fossil records from the period tell the story. Horse teeth begin to display the wear and tear associated with the use of bits. Human economies and settlement practices show signs of a rapid increase in mobility. The horse becomes a symbol of power in prehistoric art. Horse bones begin to appear in human graves.

Taken together, these changes suggest a much larger transformation, one similar to what occurred on the plains of North America in the late seventeenth century. The Cheyenne prophet Sweet Medicine explained the arrival of the horse in apocalyptic terms: buffalo would disappear from the earth and beef cattle would arrive to take their place, but between these twinned disasters, a third animal would appear, one with a "shaggy neck and a tail almost touching the ground" whose purpose was to help the tribe to find their way in the world. "Those far hills that seem only a blue vision in the distance take many days to reach," Sweet Medicine said, "but with this animal you can get there in a short time, so fear him not."

I was standing on the windblown deck of the American Legion pool when the girl rode in. In those days, a dilapidated white building, the sort of multistory monstrosity you would expect to encounter in the back streets of Saigon or Beirut, rose up on the west side of the pool, and it was across this building's ruined courtyard that the girl rode, bareback, her long legs dangling, left hand loosely encircling a hunk of mane. What a sight she was! Nymph-like and beautiful, perhaps fifteen years old (which to me was *old*, seeing as I myself was only nine or ten), the girl rode the horse with the quiet competence and non-chalance of someone who had been born on horseback.

I was instantly smitten. I remember standing there, the dry Kansas wind raising gooseflesh up and down my arms and legs, as the girl collected the horse beneath her and spun him in a cir-cle, first to the left, and then to the right, directing these balletic movements with nothing more than the pressure of her bare heels in the horse's ribs. No other part of her moved—not her head, which she held high between her shoulders, or her back or hands. Witnessing this, in the moments before the lifeguard came down from his chair to run her out of there, I remember thinking, *How is it possible that something this beautiful and profound has existed all my life, and I knew nothing about it?*

But it wasn't the girl alone that provoked this response in me. Nor was it the horse, a run-of-the-mill, aging gelding such as populated pastures for miles in every direction. Rather, it was the two of them together, rider and horse, the way they seemed to meld into each other joint and limb to form a completely new animal, an animal far more perfect and complete than either could have been without the aid of the other. The horse completed the girl, and the girl completed the horse. Seeing them together like that, I wanted them never to part.

When I arrived home from Tunisia in the summer of 1990, I weighed a little over 153 pounds—25 pounds lighter than what I had weighed as a skinny defensive back on my high school football team. My mother took one look at me and asked, "Lord God, what have they done to you?"

"Nothing that a little home cooking won't fix," I joked, trying to sound upbeat and nonchalant. In truth, I felt cynical, depleted, world-weary, and sad. Worse, I had no way of knowing how much of what I felt would be permanent, how much merely temporary.

In search of a cure, I jumped on my motorcycle and rode out to the fifteen-hundred-acre cattle ranch my father had traded for while I was off experiencing other latitudes. Topping the last hill before the ranch, I slowed the bike carefully on the sand road and paused to look down into the valley below. A tree-lined creek snaked through the middle of the property, splitting the ranch in half. On the north side of the creek, a herd of white cows grazed alongside their newborn calves. On the south side, a half mile from where I stopped to look down, a pair of horses grazed in the middle of a smaller, rockier pasture.

At first the horses stood stock still, watching me. But as I neared the gate, they came running across the pasture, front hooves reaching out before them, long tails flowing behind like kite tails. Seeing them, I felt my heart rise up in my chest. By the time the horses fetched up before the gate in a swirling cloud of dust, I was already there to greet them, my hand reaching into my coat pocket for the apple I had remembered to stow away there.

Wild Horses

We'll ride them someday . . .
—The Rolling Stones

We were on a picnic in a far-flung part of the ranch, a thousand-acre pasture called Name Rock because of the many names and dates, some of them from pioneer days, that had been carved into the limestone bluffs at the property's west end. My wife's mother, Andra, was with us that day and had offered to watch our two children, ages eight and four, if Alyssa and I wanted to go for a ride together, something we had not been able to do since before our son was born. Living in Indiana, we visited the ranch only a couple of times a year. "Let's go," I said to Alyssa as soon as I had finished my sandwich. "The horses are right here. What do you say?"

"I don't know," she responded.

Petite and tightly wound, with piercing green eyes and the abundant, frenzied energy of a dervish, my wife was a force to be reckoned with under most circumstances. Now, however, she seemed oddly tentative and nervous.

"Come on," I said. "How often does an opportunity like this come up?"

"Well, all right," she finally agreed, getting up from the picnic blanket and walking alongside me to a place along the creek where I had the horses tied up. "But I don't want to go far. It's been a long time since I've been on a horse."

"We won't go far," I assured her.

It had been five years since we had ridden together, and I was anxious to get back into it. In the early days of our courtship,

Alyssa and I had driven cross-country from western New York to western Kansas, a distance of some thirteen hundred miles, to spend a few days riding together on the ranch. Perhaps I was trying to recapture the magic of that time. It was a summer of unusually abundant rainfall, and the plains were green and alive with wildflowers. Alyssa hadn't ridden much before that; a few pony rides at Girl Scout camp was about the extent of it. After a couple of days on the ranch, however, her seat was almost as good as mine, and she had a calm about her that belied her lack of experience. Still, she was no daredevil and didn't pretend to be. "I don't care about going fast," she said. "I just want to walk and take in the countryside. That's enough for me."

As for me, I loved riding side by side across the rolling prairie, pausing here or there to allow the horses to munch on buffalo grass or drink water from the swollen creek. It made for a perfect excuse to lean across the space between us to steal a kiss. A couple of years after this memorable trip, we spent the best two days of our honeymoon on the ranch, walking and riding along the Sawlog, sending firewood up the chimney of the 1920s ranch house, drinking wine on the torch-lit front deck. My parents lived in a house in town, and so we had the place all to ourselves. One night, tipsy on champagne and wearing little more than an oversized T-shirt, Alyssa ran barefoot across the front pasture, crawled over a four-wire fence, and started up into the coyote-infested hills across Back Trail Road. When I finally caught up with her—I had stopped to pull a pair of boots onto my naked feet—and asked her what on earth she thought she was doing, she just laughed and said, "Getting closer to the moon and stars. Thanks for joining me."

That's my girl, I thought. *Wild and crazy.*

Of course, this being western Kansas, things were not always so idyllic. On subsequent trips to the ranch, we endured rattlesnakes and mosquitoes, scorching heat, fifty-mile-an-hour winds, a holiday blizzard so extreme that one couldn't stay outside more than a few minutes at a time. Still we loved being there. And though my work meant that we always lived far away—in Buffalo at first, followed by St. Louis, and finally in Indianapolis—the ranch became our special place to relax and get outside of ourselves and the grind of daily life. Horses and riding were a big part of that. I close my eyes, and the names of all the horses we rode in those days come immediately to mind. Sugar. Traveler. Daisy. Smoky. Princess. King . . . There were a couple of rebels in the bunch to keep things interesting, but for the most part they were good horses, and we had a lot of fun riding them.

After our daughter, Ria, was born, however, things began to change. We could no longer just go off by ourselves for hours or days on end. If we wanted to ride, we had to arrange for someone else, usually my mother, to look after her, something Alyssa wasn't always comfortable doing. Inevitably, our rides together grew shorter and less frequent, until finally, after our son, Jake, was born, they stopped altogether. "I just don't feel right about leaving the kids," Alyssa said. "It's too much to ask of your mother. What if something happened? I'd never forgive myself."

"What are you talking about?" I asked, frustrated. "She's their grandmother. She wants to spend time with them. Besides, riding together is important to me. Isn't it important to you?"

"You know it is," Alyssa said. "I just want to wait until the kids are a little older, that's all. You can wait that long, can't you?"

"Well, I guess," I said, giving in.

After that, I rode mostly by myself or with a few select friends, such as my brothers Dave and Joe or the hired cowboy on the ranch. In fact, I rode more than ever, often three or four hours at a time.

Sometimes, coming back from a ride, I would find Alyssa and the kids waiting for me in the corrals below the tack barn, Alyssa in her running shoes, flanked on both sides by the ranch dogs that followed her wherever she went. "The kids want you to take them on a ride now," she would say, and I would lift them onto the backs of a couple of horses and lead them around while Alyssa went on a run to Owl Rock and back. Both kids loved riding from the first. Once, during a week my daughter and I spent together on the ranch while Alyssa and Jake remained home in Indianapolis, I borrowed an old mule named Johann from a friend of my father's, and Ria, who was six or seven years old at the time, got to ride by herself in the big pasture. On the way home to Indiana, I thought I'd never hear the end of that mule.

"Johann is the best. I could ride him all the way to California and back, no problem."

"I take it you like riding?" I asked.

"Are you *kidding?*" she said, playing along. "I absolutely *adore* it."

"I'm glad," I said. "So do I."

On the day of our family picnic at Name Rock, I saw to it that we trailered a couple of horses with us to the pasture, just in case an opportunity to ride surfaced. When it did, in the form of my mother-in-law's offer to watch the kids, I quickly adjusted the stirrups on an old ranch horse named Leo, helped Alyssa into the saddle, and off we went.

It was a gorgeous, unseasonably warm day with clear skies and just enough wind to keep the gnats and mosquitoes at bay. We rode up a short, rocky slope to a stretch of flat land above, talking quietly as we rode, just as we had in days gone by. We were on our way now, turning back the clock to a simpler, crazier, less responsible time.

"I don't want to go far," Alyssa reminded me.

"Don't worry, we won't," I responded.

Nearing the top of the pasture, at the place where I planned to begin circling back to the picnic site, Leo began to shake his head and prance sideways. Then he trotted ahead a little.

"Turn him back this way," I called to Alyssa.

"I'm trying to," she called back. "He won't listen."

"Turn him," I said again. "Bring his nose to your knee if you have to."

By now, trotting faster, Leo had reached the very top of the rise. The entrance to the pasture, just across the road from a field in which five or six broodmares grazed alongside their foals, rose suddenly into view. I watched as Alyssa tried once more to bring her horse's nose around, away from this distraction. She almost had it when, with a single jerk of his powerful neck, Leo pulled the reins out of her hands and took off across the plains at a gallop.

"Rob!" Alyssa called out. "Rob! Help me!"

Putting spurs to Cuba, the palomino I was riding, I took off after them at a dead run, but the best I could do was to keep the gap between us from widening. Alyssa held tight to the saddle horn, her body hunched over in an intense balancing act, like a stuntman perched atop a runaway train. As the horses ran on and Leo lengthened his stride, I looked ahead to the far end of the pasture, a plan beginning to form in my mind. When we reached the end of the pasture and Leo pulled up short before the four-wire fence, I would jump off my horse and grab the fallen reins before he could take off again.

However, he didn't stop. Instead he ran *straight through* the fence, pulling a couple of heavy posts out of the ground and dragging them behind him across the road. I followed them through the hole in the gate at a dead run. Crossing the road, we came to an abandoned farmstead, where I lost them briefly behind the weedy corrals and the barn. When I caught up a moment later, Alyssa was lying on the hard-packed ground near the entrance to the corrals, and Leo, riderless now, was making his way down the fence line to the field across the creek where the mares were grazing alongside their foals. Sliding to a stop, I dropped Cuba's reins and ran to where Alyssa lay on the ground.

"Are you all right?"

"Where am I?" she asked, rubbing the side of her head.

"On the ranch," I said. "Are you okay?"

"I don't know," she said, sounding confused. "Where are the kids?"

"They're with your mother. Don't you remember?"

"I guess so," she said, uncertainly.

"Did you fall off the horse or jump off?" I asked. "How did you land? Did you hit your head?"

"I don't remember," she said.

Just then, Leo came trotting up from the creek. I helped Alyssa to her feet and stepped away long enough to grab the horse's reins. He looked calm and unconcerned, as though nothing had happened. Suppressing an urge to whip him across the face with the reins, I led him back to where I had left Alyssa and Cuba.

"How do you feel?" I asked. "Do you think you can walk?"

"I don't know," Alyssa said, looking wobbly and disoriented. "I can try, I guess."

We began the long walk back to the picnic site. I had to hold Alyssa up by her shoulders with one arm while I led the horses with the other. Every twenty yards or so, we stopped to rest.

"Where am I?" she asked every few minutes. "What happened? Where are the kids?"

"In Dodge," I reminded her. "You fell off a horse, but the kids are fine. We'll be with them soon."

Two hours later, in the emergency room of Dodge City Regional Hospital, a doctor in a cowboy hat and boots confirmed what I had already guessed: Alyssa had hit her head coming off the horse and now had a category two concussion. "She'll recover just fine," the doctor said, looking over the results of her brain scan and x-rays. "Of course, she'll need to take it easy for a couple of months. No riding or anything else that might jar the brain."

"Can I jog?" Alyssa asked.

"She goes running a couple of miles every morning," I said.

"Well, not right away," the doctor said. "You could get dizzy and fall again. That's the real danger—a second concussion on top of the first one. I'd give it at least a month, and then see how you feel."

"Oh," Alyssa said, sounding vacant and defeated.

As for the episode itself, she had little memory of that beyond the terror she felt when the horse took off with her. However, that is not to say she had no opinion about what had happened. "You put me on that horse," she said in a kind of monotone, after the doctor left us.

"I know I did," I said. "I'm sorry. I didn't know . . ."

"You couldn't *stop* him," she said. "I used to believe you could rescue me no matter what happened. But now I know you can't. I mean, you're the one who put me on that horse in the first place."

"I know that," I said. "I know I did."

It goes without saying that horses are highly strung, volatile animals. Spend enough time around them and the question is not *if* some wreck will happen but *when* and *how bad* it will be. I knew this better than most. On my mother's side of the family alone, there were ample examples. Throughout her childhood in the Flint Hills, my mother's grandfather was known around town as the man who'd been "kicked in the head by a horse and never the same since." Her brother Danny died in part because of injuries he'd sustained after being bucked off a colt in Colorado. My mother herself had had both arms broken in an accident involving a runaway horse-drawn buggy. As for me, in twenty-five years of riding, I had been bitten, kicked, stepped on, bucked down, and run off with more times than I cared to remember.

Alyssa had shared in some of this history. Riding on the ranch, she had encountered her share of difficult horses and had even had one run away with her. However, what happened at Name Rock was more complicated and scary than that because, as Alyssa continued to point out, once Leo got the reins away from her and took off, I had been powerless to do anything about it.

You put me on that horse . . .

These words haunted me throughout the five or six weeks it took Alyssa to recover enough to resume her morning runs on the golf course near our home in Indianapolis.

Even more, I was haunted by the things I might have done *before* the horse ran off. I could have listened better and let Alyssa decide when she was ready to ride again, instead of giving way to impatience and rushing her. I could have brought her along more slowly, seeing to it that she practiced in the corrals before attempting to ride in a pasture as big and wide open as Name Rock. I could have demonstrated for her, as I had in years past, how to stop a running horse by pulling its head around to its shoulder (the so-called one-rein stop). I could have ridden Leo more in the days and hours leading up to the accident, paying closer attention to his mood (especially once he had spotted those mares), or at the very least made sure he was good and worn out before Alyssa ever got on him. I could have tied his head down and put a curb bit in his mouth, instead of letting him get his neck high and his teeth clenched on a bit that lacked stopping power. I could have led him on a rope from my horse or left him behind altogether, Alyssa and I riding double on Cuba. I could have done all of these things and many more besides, but the fact was I hadn't, and that was something I was just going to have to learn to live with over the long haul, perhaps forever.

As bad as all this was, far worse was seeing how much the episode had affected Alyssa. Being around horses—or even hearing me talk about them on the phone with one of my brothers—brought the episode with Leo back to her in vivid, painful ways. On especially bad days, she had flashbacks of a sort in which she relived the experience all over again. Once, on a field trip to a riding stable with a troop of Girl Scouts, the stable owner, unfamiliar with Alyssa's history with horses, asked her to help lead some of the girls around the indoor arena. Anyone else would have begged off or got another parent to do it, but making excuses had never been Alyssa's style, and so she gritted her teeth and got through it. Afterward, she said, "Just being in that stable, just seeing those horses, brought it all back. It was like I was on Leo all over again, terrified, seeing my life flash before my eyes." And here she paused to fix me with those sorrowful green eyes of hers. "I could have died, you know. The whole time, I felt like I was going to die."

"I'm sorry," I said, for what felt like the fiftieth time. "What else do you want me to say?"

"I don't mean to put a guilt trip on you," she said after a pause. "It's just that I need you to hear and understand what I'm saying. I need to know you're not going to rush me back onto a horse. I'm not ready. I don't know if I'll ever *be* ready."

"I know all that," I said. "Look, it's *you* I care about, not whether or not you get on a horse again."

"Are you sure?"

"Yes," I said. "Of course I'm sure."

I meant every word. And yet, even as I encouraged Alyssa to step back from horses and riding, I found myself taking several steps forward. At about this time, my brother Joe began to get into horses in a very big way, and I spent a lot of time on the phone with him talking about everything from breeds and saddles to trailers, barns, and farrier bills. On sabbatical from my teaching position, I read everything about horses and riding that I could get my hands on, beginning with Xenophon's *The Art of Horsemanship,* a work dating from 350 BC. I ordered videos and studied the websites of modern clinicians such as Pat Parelli, Clinton Anderson, and Craig Cameron. I even signed up for riding lessons at a stable half an hour from my house, learning all over again how to saddle, halter, and lead a horse, how to control its feet from the ground with a longe line and whip, how to post in the saddle, ride a reining pattern, change leads on the fly, and so on. I told myself I was starting over from scratch—no skipping over anything, no mistakes.

My instructor, a woman half my age with a degree in equine science, had few complaints about how I sat or stayed on a horse. "I'm afraid I have nothing to teach you in that regard," she said. At the same time, she expressed amazement that someone could have ridden as long as I had and still not possess any idea of how to collect a horse or start it out on the correct lead. "Along with safety stuff, that's Horse 101," she said.

"Good," I replied. "That's exactly what I want. Horse 101."

As I progressed in these lessons, I brought a lot of what I was learning to bear on the situation at the ranch, buying new and better tack for the horses, as well as helmets for Ria and Jake to wear as I began to take the first steps toward teaching them to ride. I told myself I wanted them to learn to ride the right way, not the way I had learned growing up. At the same time, I made sure they got to ride bareback a lot in the big corral so they could experience the feeling of a horse's body moving beneath them, that muscle-on-muscle, bone-on-bone feeling that made it possible to believe you were part of the horse and could no more fall off than the horse's ears or hide could.

Often, while we were at these lessons, Alyssa would stop by on her way back from her morning run. As she stood outside the corral watching the kids perform some simple maneuver they had just learned, I stood inside the corral watching her, wondering whether any part of the fear that gripped her was loosening its hold.

Be patient, I told myself. *She'll decide when she's ready. And if she doesn't . . . Well, that will have to be okay, too.*

In December 2008, three years after Alyssa's accident, we spent the week between Christmas and New Year's on the Lazy R. It was our longest stay there in four or five years, and the weather was spectacular the entire week, more like spring or Indian summer than winter. By then, Leo and several of the other ranch horses were gone, and my brothers Joe and Dave had begun to put together a stable of new horses, a couple of them tame enough for Ria and Jake to ride with supervision. One of these horses, a sorrel gelding named Jack, became a great favorite of Ria's. She rode him all week long, both in the corrals and in the alfalfa patch between the corrals and the west pasture. In many ways, Jack was a throwback to some of the horses we'd had on the place when Alyssa and I first started riding together fifteen years before. He had plenty of power and speed when you asked for it, but as soon as you stopped asking, he slowed right back down. He was almost perfect in that way, and of course both Ria and I raved about him. All week long, it was Jack this, and Jack that.

One afternoon toward the end of that week, while the kids and I were in the corral putting Jack through his paces, Alyssa walked over from the ranch house and stood watching from the gate to the corral.

"So is this the famous Jack I've been hearing so much about?" she asked.

"It is," I said. "Do you want to meet him?"

"All right."

Pushing the gate open, she came over to where Ria stood holding Jack's reins and began to rub him along his neck and face.

"I'm still a little nervous around them," she said. "Do you think Jack can tell?"

"I don't know," I said. "He looks pretty calm to me."

There followed a brief pause, and then Alyssa said, "Maybe I'll get up on him and have you lead me around a little, the way you do with the kids."

"Are you sure?" I asked.

"Yes," she said. "But let's do it right now, before I lose my nerve and chicken out."

After handing her Ria's helmet, I adjusted the saddle and watched as she climbed up. "How do you feel?" I asked.

"Okay."

"No panic or fear?"

"No, none of that," she said. "I just worry the horse won't respect or listen to me."

I nodded and began to lead her in a big circle around the corral. "Jack's not Leo," I said after a while. "I could be wrong, but I think he'd listen fine."

After a couple of times around the corral, Alyssa said she wanted to ride double a little, so I got up in front of her, and together we rode Jack in a big circle. I can't describe how good it felt to be on that horse with Alyssa's arms wrapped tightly around my waist. In the three years since the accident, I had more or less given up hope that it would ever happen. I told myself I couldn't expect it and that maybe I didn't deserve it. But now it was happening, and all I could do was smile.

"I'm just taking it slow," Alyssa said into my ear.

"That's fine," I said. "I like slow."

A few months after this, during the kids' spring break, we returned to the ranch to spend another long week. Again the weather was nearly perfect. I rode a lot, and so did the kids, but we also hiked and went on picnics in the Jeep. During the evenings, I noticed that Alyssa had begun reading a couple of the books I had bought a few years before, during my reeducation in horsemanship. She even began to give little reports on these books for the benefit of the rest of us. "Horses are prey animals," she said. "They react to fear by running. Riding a horse is all about communication and trust."

"Is that so?" I asked.

"Yes, it is."

At the end of that week, after a few practice sessions in the corral, Alyssa announced that she was ready to go for a ride on Jack. "Just a short one," she said. "To Owl Rock and back. At a walk."

"Whatever you say," I responded, struggling to hold back a smile.

It was late in the evening, that time on the ranch when the wind dies to a whisper and the shadows thrown by everything from towering buttes to fence posts grow long across the land. Keeping the horses at a walk, we rode across the expansive, undulating pasture until we came to the chalky bluff we had named Owl Rock after the bird that sometimes perched in a hole in the face of the outcropping in the years when we first started coming to the ranch from Buffalo. We had not seen this bird in several years and sometimes speculated on what might have happened to it and whether another bird might appear to take its place. Despite this speculation, it was a little startling to both of us when, rounding a corner in the road below the bluff, the great shadow of a bird passed over us, followed by the bird itself.

"Did you just see what I saw?" I asked.

"I did," Alyssa said. "Do you think it was him?"

"I don't know," I answered. "It might be another one. Either way, it's good to see him, don't you think?"

"I do," Alyssa agreed.

After riding up and over the top of the bluff, we turned and walked the horses in the direction of the ranch house, our shadows falling long and lean behind us.

Feedlot Cowboy

I set the alarm on my cell phone for 3:45 a.m., but anticipation had me up and throwing hay to the horses half an hour before that. Bill Hommertzheim, manager of the southwestern Kansas feedlot where I planned to spend the day as a pen rider, had told me to report for work at 6:30 sharp, and since the ranch was every bit of a hundred miles away, I knew I'd have to get an early start if I was going to make it on time. While the horses ate, I checked over the saddles and other tack I had loaded onto the flatbed of the ranch truck the evening before. I was nervous in that way one gets when hurrying to make a flight at a far-off airport. Had I left myself enough time? What if I forgot something or had a flat tire? Beneath this veneer of nervousness, however, I felt a deeper layer of raw excitement for what I was about to do, together with a kind of smug satisfaction that it was I and no one else who had come up with the idea.

Half an hour later, I had entered a thick fog on the correction line between Dodge City and Cimarron. The blacktop was narrow and unmarked. Within ten seconds of entering the full thickness of the fog, I could see maybe a hundred feet in front of me. I had to downshift from fifth to third just to keep the truck out of the ditch. Leaning over the truck's steering wheel, I rubbed at the inside of the filthy windshield with a shop rag, hoping to work some kind of miracle. At the rate I was going, I would reach the feedlot at 7:00 a.m. or later, thus proving to Bill and whatever help he had assembled there that I wasn't even capable of showing up to work on time, let alone riding pens and scouting cattle for disease or other trouble.

The idea had come to me a few days before, when my family and I were headed west from Kansas City on one of our frequent visits to the cattle ranch my parents owned northeast of Dodge City. Somewhere near Emporia, we happened to drive past a big commercial feedlot—one of those massive, open-air animal feeding operations ("AFO" is the industry acronym) where tens of thousands of head of cattle are fed a steady diet of corn and antibiotics in the months before they are shipped to slaughter.

"God, what's that smell?!" my teenage daughter said, fanning the air in front of her nose with the paperback she was reading. My son, all of ten, looked out his window and asked, in that way he still had that assumed I possessed the answers to everything, who those men were and what they were doing out there.

"What men?" I asked.

"*Those.*" He pointed out the window. "Are they cowboys?"

I craned my head to see what he was talking about. Here and there amid the acres of penned cattle, a few solitary figures with wide-brimmed straw hats could be seen moving about on horseback.

"Pen riders," I told him. "Feedlot cowboys."

"Are they *real* cowboys?"

"I don't know. I guess that depends on what you think a real cowboy is."

Here the boy sighed, impatient with the wishy-washiness of the answer. "Come on, Dad. Just tell me. Are they real or not?"

"All right, they're real," I said. "No question about it. Satisfied?"

"Yes," he answered, his attention already shifting from the feedlot to the gunfire and explosions taking place on his Gameboy.

I thought that would be the end of it, but as we continued on our way, I lingered over the question. What was a real cowboy—especially in this day and age? What qualified a person to be called by the name? Was it a question of clothes, attitude, allegiance to some idea or other? Surely a mastery of horses came into the equation somewhere. Cattle, too, obviously. After all, historically speaking, wasn't the herding and safe delivery of cattle the cowboy's whole reason for existing? Gradually, a definition of sorts began to form itself at the front of my brain. *A cowboy is someone who tends cattle from horseback every day of his working life.* The precision and tidiness of the definition pleased me. Of course, by this standard, almost none of the people I knew, including several who spent tens of thousands of dollars a year on horses and tack, were real cowboys. I myself didn't come close to qualifying. Did I even want to? It was an interesting question.

"What are you thinking about now?" my wife asked after a couple of miles. "I don't like the look you're starting to get on your face."

"What look?" I asked.

"You know the one," she said. "Devious grin, eyebrows raised, ideas sprouting willy-nilly."

"I don't know what you're talking about," I said.

That evening, after we made it to the ranch, I called Bill Hommertzheim, a relative by marriage of my older brother Dave, and asked him what he thought about my riding pens for a day at the feedlot he managed near Scott City.

"I don't give a shit," Bill said in that blunt way he had, as if there were no man living who was smarter and tougher than he was, and the rest of the world had better get used to it. "I'll tell you what, though," he continued. "You've got to pull your weight and put in a full day's work. No taking little *writing breaks,* or cutting out of here early, or shit like that. You got to *toe the line,* just like all the rest of us. You don't, and we'll sure as hell run you off the place."

I could feel myself bristling inwardly at the challenge contained in these words, which I knew to be more than half bluster.

"Oh, I'll pull my weight," I said. "Don't worry about that."

"Good!" Bill said. "We'll see you at 6:30 sharp."

At 5:40, with seventy-five miles still left to go, my prayers were answered, and the fog began to lift. A few miles after that, I turned north on a good, two lane road, and the fog dropped away completely. I shifted up from third to fifth, putting the hammer down on the pickup's 24-valve Cummins engine.

Now we're getting somewhere, I thought.

I felt like William Hazlitt in his essay "The Fight," or maybe Ivan Turgenev in "The Execution of Tropmann." I would go and I would witness, and what I witnessed would become . . . well, we would see about that, wouldn't we?

Among ranchers of my father's generation, Bill Hommertz-heim will forever be "Homer" or "Homey," a hardworking kid who played some football for St. Mary of the Plains College in Dodge City before learning the feedlot trade and perfecting it with that mad science for organization and attention to detail all Germans from farm backgrounds carry inside themselves like a disease. Never mind that Bill is closer to sixty than fifty, and sorely in need of double knee replacement surgery, and talks a little more than is seemly for a true died-in-the-wool German. He is still Homer for all that, a hero of both the grid-iron and the feedlot, a rare accomplishment indeed.

Depending on which side of the legend you believe, the Great American Cowboy who came north with herds of Texas longhorns in the 1870s and 1880s was either a violent, hard-drinking, pistol-toting miscreant or else a congenial, soft-spoken "cavalier of the plains" who understood horses and cattle and was unfailingly kind to women and small children. It goes without saying that both halves of the legend are bogus. Historical cowboys were defined not by personality traits or social versus antisocial tendencies but rather by the dirty, demanding work they performed. Common laborers, they were typically drawn from the ranks of the destitute and poor, and a fair number of them (as many as one in three, according to some estimates) were Mexican or African American. Many more were Civil War vets already well acquainted with hardship and deprivation. As the cowboy Teddy "Blue" Abbott noted in his memoir of the trail, *We Pointed Them North* (1939), the average trail hand was "raised under just the same conditions as there was on the trail—corn meal and bacon for grub, dirt floors in the houses, no luxuries." They were men who liked to brag that they could "go any place a cow could" and "stand anything a horse could," which is to say they took a strange pride in all of the suffering they endured.

A lot of this had changed by the time Bill was growing up on a farm in central Kansas in the 1950s and '60s. The open range had been replaced by fenced pastures; the old longhorn steer with its trail-toughened meat by Angus and Hereford cattle with their marbled, succulent flesh; the tiny but hardy Spanish cow pony by bigger quarter horses bred for the show and competition ring. As for Homer, he dreamed of being a football star and maybe a high school coach, not a cowboy. However, to pay his tuition bill at St. Mary of the Plains, he did cowboy some, hiring out on a part-time basis at feedlots that were then springing up in a fifty-mile radius of Dodge, an experience he describes as educational in a how-not-to-do-things sort of way.

"It was awful in a lot of ways," Bill says, shaking his head. "The whole feedlot business was just starting out, and nobody knew a goddamn thing about how to keep that many animals in one place and keep them alive. Nobody knew how to ride a pen, or what to look for, or even whether or not a horse should even play a part in the work. There was no system to it at all, just cattle, chaos, and wild swings of fortune depending on all kinds of things that were out of our control. I was working at one of the bigger outfits when the Blizzard of 1978 hit. You have no idea of the destruction that caused. You needed a loader and a dump truck just to haul away the corpses. We had no idea how to doctor them either. One cow got sick, they all got sick. I'm telling you, it was just death, death, death."

That's where Bill's special talent came into play—a talent that exceeded even his prowess at football. "One summer when I was a kid," he says, recounting a favorite story, "my aunt gave me a bunch of chickens to raise as fryers. A neighbor took one look at the box of chicks and said, 'Don't waste your time. They're all gonna get sick and die.' I said to him, 'You wanna bet? I can keep these sumbitches alive. Just you wait and see.'"

Here Bill grins, remembering. "I didn't know a goddamn thing about chickens, but I was determined. I kept my eye on those birds 24/7, wracking my brains night and day thinking about what might happen to them and how I could prevent it. Long story short, when the end of the summer came and my aunt showed up to get her fryers, I hadn't lost a single bird. Not one, you understand? Well, my aunt looked at them birds, all fat and healthy, and said, 'Goddamn, Billy! How'd you do it?' 'It wasn't hard,' I said. 'You just have to pay attention.' Very few people pay attention to anything these days."

It was this talent that Bill carried into his part-time job at the feedlot. But when the time came for him to do his student teaching, he faced a dilemma of sorts. "They don't pay you for that," he says. "I had bills to pay, and I needed the teaching experience to get certified, but how was I going to get the experience if I starved to death in the meantime?" He throws his hand out before him like a punch, dismissing the memory. "I kept on at the feedlot, even after I graduated with my degree in education."

A year or two into his feedlot career, Bill could feel a door closing behind him. He would have made a good teacher and a better coach, but other work had claimed him, as it claims so many of us. The feedlot had entered his bloodstream. It was who he was now. Like the other pen riders, he wore a cowboy hat and boots and maintained a string of ponies to use at work. In time, he even developed his own system for how to ride a pen, what to look for and what to ignore, when to pull a cow from the herd and send it to the hospital, when to let it go another day or two. There was deep satisfaction in this work, yes, but did any of it make him a cowboy?

"You got to understand," Bill says when asked this question. "My idea of a cowboy was John Wayne. I thought well enough of myself. But John Wayne? The Duke? That's setting the bar pretty high . . ."

Hearing Bill say this, one gets the impression that in his case maybe the bar wasn't set *all* that high, Duke or no Duke.

After all, there is image and then there is reality, and the world of the feedlot is all about reality, day in and day out, 24/7.

By the time I rolled through Scott City, eight miles east of the feedlot, the pickup's digital clock read 6:32. The world was still gray-dark outside, and from what I could see, the land in all directions was flat as a tabletop. There were no trees to speak of, and hardly any farmhouses or other buildings—just wheat and corn stubble and the occasional pasture dotted with cattle, the roads running between these giant fields as straight and true as if someone had drawn them with a straightedge. I caught the smell of the feedlot before I saw anything. First a big one loomed on the right side of the road, and then Bill's, somewhat smaller, came up on my left. It was a big, flat, industrial space, nothing but pen after pen of milling, bawling cattle, with a noisy feed mill towering over one end and greenish-black wastewater ponds at the other. Light poles illuminated the scale house and the wide gravel lot at the center of the place, throwing an eerie fluorescent glow on everything, reminding me of one of those lunar mining scenes you sometimes see in science fiction movies.

Bill met me in the carpeted hallway of the feedlot's main office, a bunker-like building with a bathroom, a couple of desks with computer equipment, and a massive scale for weighing trucks. "How the hell are you? Are you ready to go to work?" he asked, his eyes inspecting me over the tops of wire-rim glasses. He looked older than the last time I had seen him but still hale and forceful for all that, every bit the retired footballer in cowboy boots and a XXXX Stetson.

"I'm good," I said. "How are your knees? Dave tells me you're looking at a double replacement."

"When I can get *time*, I am." Bill glanced at his watch dramatically, as if to comment on my tardiness. "Got an interesting day lined up for you. Think you're ready?"

"You bet."

"Come on, then," he told me. "I'll take you down to the barn and introduce you to Apache and the boys."

The barn was a squat metal building set on hardpan in the dead center of the feedlot. I parked the ranch truck on a wide gravel lot next to the building and unloaded the horses: Cuba, a ten-year-old palomino gelding that according to Bill had been "ruined by too much roping," and Doc, a seven-year-old sorrel gelding my brother Joe had recently acquired from a man who said the horse had spent several years working in a feedlot. I saddled them quickly and led them to a pipe rail behind the barn, where four other horses stood tied, then joined Bill and the rest of the crew inside.

Snaking from one end of the barn to the other was a taper-sided crowd alley leading to a hydraulic squeeze chute. Overhead doors opened on three sides of the building, allowing a manure-tinged breeze to whisper through. Dozens of small birds nested in the rafters above the concrete floor, providing a discordant soundtrack to the place. In a corner of the building closest to where the horses were tied, a metal door opened to a small break/supply room with lockers and a big, glass-fronted refrigerator full of antibiotics and other drugs.

"This is Joaquin, also known as Apache," Bill said, indicating a tall man in his mid-thirties with steady brown eyes, high cheekbones, and jet-black hair cut into a Mohawk. "Apache's been with me the longest of all these guys. What is it now, Apach? Eight years?"

"Yes, eight," Joaquin answered, reaching out to shake my hand.

"These other guys are Jose, been with me six years, Sergio, and Jaime," Bill continued as I shook each man's hand in turn. Ranging in age from nineteen to thirty, the men were all dressed in cheap, durable work clothes—feed caps, jeans bought at Wal-Mart, cotton hoodies—whereas I, by contrast, had on a straw cowboy hat, a long-sleeved Roper shirt with pearl buttons, and a pair of leather rodeo chaps.

"You'll find that none of these boys says very much," Bill said, hand on my shoulder, very coach-like. "At least not in *English*. But just stick by Apache, and he'll tell you what to do." He handed Joaquin a to-do list full of pen numbers and head counts and feeding regimes, and turned back to me one final time. "Any questions?"

"Yeah, what time is lunch?" I said, attempting a joke.

"After all the pens are ridden," Bill said over his shoulder, already on his way out the door and back to his office in the scale house.

After Bill was gone, Jose offered me a seat and a cup of coffee, and the five of us sat around a while in the polite, awkward silence of people who have been thrown together but do not speak the same language. There was a lot of eye contact and nodding smiles. A donut was offered, which I declined. There was so much I wanted to ask these men, I didn't know where to begin.

I wanted to ask: Are you legal? Do you like your job? How much are you paid? Do you have health insurance? How did you learn to ride? Do you consider yourself a cowboy? Do you consider this place where you work a fucking environmental disaster area? Do you have kids? What are your dreams for them? Do they play too many video games and eat too much sugary cereal? What are the best and worst parts of your day? Do you like cattle, or are they just meat to you? Do you love horses?

In the end, though, I just sat there with a dumb smile glued to my face, nodding and supplying the answers myself.

"Okay," Joaquin said, having finished the Marlboro he was smoking. "Now we go get the cattle."

We grabbed bridles, pulled tight the cinches on our saddles, and mounted. By now the sun was up. It was a misty morning, chilly for late May. Leaving the barn, we rode down a sand alley as wide as any city street. Not a blade of grass grew anywhere. The whole place was nothing but sand and mud, fourteen-gauge steel pipe, and cattle, cattle, cattle. Black cattle, brown cattle, yellow cattle, white cattle. Big and not so big, heifers and steers. Thousands upon thousands of them, all standing around in the sand and mud, waiting for breakfast, which even then was being delivered by trucks making runs from the feed mill to the concrete feed bunks lining the pens.

Sergio and Jaime rode ahead to open a series of gates, which Jose and Joaquin and I chained together to form a single, L-shaped alley leading from the far end of the feedlot back to the processing barn. Cuba, a bundle of energy as always, tossed his head and danced excitedly down the middle of the alley, calling into question my ability to control him.

"Nice horse," Joaquin offered, nodding appreciatively.

"He's a good horse," I agreed. "A little crazy, though. *Caballo loco?*"

"*Si, caballo loco.*" Jose laughed. "All palominos are that way."

Five minutes after leaving the barn, we came to the first pen on Bill's work order. Joaquin, leaning sideways from his horse, opened the gate and held it for me as I rode through. The simple grace with which he performed this maneuver—no motion or effort wasted, the entire thing a single, fluid movement—filled me with professional envy. Did I have a right to that envy? I didn't know. All I knew was that I wanted my own horsemanship to be like that. What would it take to get there? How many repetitions over how many days and weeks? It was a little daunting to think of, although still squarely in the realm of possibility. There was no question that Cuba was capable. But was I?

Once in the pen, we began a slow, methodical gathering of the one hundred or so cattle it contained. Moving no faster than our horses carried us at a walk, we slowly pushed the cattle out of the pen and into the alley we had built to funnel them back to the processing barn. Jaime, Jose, and Sergio rode at the point of our herd, while Joaquin and I brought up the rear.

"When did these cattle get here?" I asked Joaquin.

"Yesterday," he answered.

"How long will they stay?"

"Six months, maybe. Until they're fat."

"What's fat?"

"Twelve hundred pounds, maybe."

"How much do they weight now?"

"Seven or eight hundred."

I paused to do the math. "So they gain what, five hundred pounds in six months?"

"A little more. The goal is three and a half pounds a day."

"That's a lot of corn," I observed.

"Yes," Joaquin agreed, smiling for the first time that day. "A lot of corn."

After herding the first group of cows into pens behind the processing barn, we rode out to the next pen on Bill's list and brought these cattle in the same way. Two more times we repeated the operation, riding out to distant parts of the roughly 640-acre yard and slowly trailing the cattle in. By the second trip, I had begun to help with the opening and closing of gates. By the fourth, Cuba had dropped his head and settled into the work. The sun had burned through the early morning mist by then. The sky was a dull gray above the level horizon. Feed trucks rumbled up and down the sand alleyways, delivering the morning ration of corn and silage.

With a capacity of 16,000 head, the feedlot contained five or six times the number of cows in the average herd of longhorns driven up the trail to Dodge City in the 1870s and 1880s. Still, it was a fairly small yard by industry standards. A half an hour to the west was a corporate-owned yard with a capacity of over 100,000 head. Another yard to the south fed 120,000 head. Veritable cities of cattle, these megayards called to mind the sprawl, crowded conditions, and large-scale pollution of a Mumbai or Mexico City. But even the relatively small feedlot we were riding had some of this feel. The feed mill was the size of a small office building, and the removal of manure from the pens was a gargantuan task involving the use of loaders and dump trucks. From this densely complex environment an equally complex smell arose: a mixture of corn silage, cow manure, and an evil-smelling gas that was especially strong the closer one got to the black lagoons holding runoff from the pens.

By 7:15, we had gathered the last of the cattle on Bill's work order. I tied Cuba to his place at the pipe rail behind the barn, loosened his cinch, and followed Joaquin into the break room, where Jose and Sergio were drinking coffee and Jaime, seated at a table in the corner, was busy pressing lot numbers onto a stack of rubber ear tags.

I shot a look to Jose, as if to ask, "Now what?"

"Process cattle," he said, sipping at the steaming coffee.

Back in trail drive days, working cattle meant gathering them from the open range and separating the calves from the rest of the herd. One by one, these calves were roped, dragged to a fire, and branded. If the calf was male, it was castrated. If it had horns that could injure another cow, these were cut off with a hacksaw or a pair of heavy clippers. The principal tools in this work were the lariat or rope, the branding iron, and the castrating knife, and even novice cowboys quickly became adept in the use of all three. With the exception of the knife, today's feedlot cowboy has no use for any of this. His "range" is a world of numbered pens and concrete-floored processing barns, and his tools are a crowd alley and squeeze chute, an implant gun for the injection of growth hormones, and, above all, a jumbo hypodermic syringe for the delivery of antibiotics and other drugs.

This is the hidden, vaguely obscene world few Americans know anything about. In theory, yes, they know it exists. An extensive archive of activist videos awaits anyone who cares to get on YouTube to take a peek. But most people prefer not to know, or at least not to think about, where their food comes from. Growing up amid farm and ranch work, I had never had that luxury, and so, in a sense, I suffered from the opposite problem. Continued exposure to ranch and farm life had hardened me to it the way an ER doctor becomes hardened to the sight of blood and amputated limbs. To really *see* the world of the feedlot in all its postmodern bizarreness was an effort for me. I had to continually ask myself, *What in this picture would strike my vegan colleagues at the university as especially evil and strange?* and even then I mostly failed. We are who we are, as Homer liked to say.

As we prepared to process the cattle we had gathered that morning, Joaquin arranged tagging knife and ear tags, antiseptic wash, hormone implants, and other necessities on a little cart he wheeled into place beside the squeeze chute. Every man on the crew had a job. One man drove the cattle up the crowd alley. Another caught the cattle one by one in the hydraulic squeeze chute and gave them a couple of quick injections. A third, working on the opposite side of the chute, cut excess hair from tails (so great balls of mud wouldn't form there after a few days in the pens) and reached a gloved hand between the hind legs to make sure the males had been castrated. Joaquin, working at the front of the chute, gave each cow an implant beneath the skin of its left ear.

My job was to attach a rubber ID tag to the same ear. "Hold the tag on the knife with your thumb," Joaquin instructed me in his quiet way. "Then take the ear in your left hand, slice the tag up and through the ear, release your thumb, and pull the knife back out like this, leaving the tag in. See?"

I did see. The question was whether I could do it myself without botching the job. Another cow was driven into the chute. I placed a tag on the tiny nub of metal at the end of the tagging knife and waited for Joaquin to finish with the implant. Then I stepped in, grabbed the cow's ear, and sliced up and through it as Joaquin had shown me. However, when I removed the knife, the tag came out, too, falling at my feet on the dirty concrete floor. Looking up at where the tag should have been, I saw only an L-shaped hole in the cow's ear with blood dripping from it.

"You have to *let go* with your thumb," Joaquin said, picking up the tag from the floor and skillfully slicing it into a different part of the ear.

"Okay," I said. "I think I've got it now."

Another cow was driven into the chute. This time I let go with my thumb at the right moment, and the tag, though loose and bloody, stayed in. I stepped back, Joaquin checked my work, and the cow was released into a holding pen outside the barn.

Over and over I repeated the task, sometimes performing it flawlessly, more often mucking it up in some small or big way. By the time I had tagged twelve or fifteen cattle, my right thumb began to ache from the strain of holding the tag in place on the knife. After thirty, both of my hands ached, and I could feel the concrete floor coming up through the heels of my boots. Still the cattle kept coming, one after another. I concentrated on simplifying the motions involved in the task, so I would have more time to relax the muscles in my hands between animals. I made sure to dry my fingers on a paper towel, so that grasping the next cow's ear would be a little easier. Throughout all this, I could feel the eyes of Joaquin and the other men on me. They were sizing me up, seeing whether this professor could hack it in their world. The more blood-smeared my thirty-dollar cowboy shirt became, the more they smiled and winked at each other. I did not blame them in the least for this. From what I could tell, the job of processing cattle was a case of carpal tunnel waiting to happen. It was like working on an assembly line—or in a beef packing plant. I kept asking myself, *How do they do it? How do they keep coming back for this punishment, day after day after day?* But no answer was forthcoming.

"Getting tired?" Joaquin asked with a grin, after we had processed a hundred cattle.

"A little," I said. "How about you?"

He shrugged in his stoic way, and I dug my cell phone out of my shirt pocket and glanced at the screen. Sweet Jesus! 8:45 a.m.! Back home in Indianapolis, I would be propped up in bed with the newspaper and a cup of coffee, quietly contemplating the day to come.

Bill is the only white American working at his feedlot; the rest of the feedlot staff, from the pen riders to the feed truck drivers to the front office help, are Mexican. When I asked Bill why this was, he gave me a level look and said, "The day when you could get a white man to do this job is over, son. Or if you can, you better watch out for what kind of white man he is. Pretty soon, he starts showing up to work drunk or hung over. Then things start to go missing in the supply room, and you have to starting keeping everything under lock and key. And don't even get me started on lawsuits and worker's comp . . ."

Here Bill pauses. "I had this one kid come out and apply. Good-looking kid, strong and clean-cut, would have made an excellent linebacker. Halfway through the interview, I'm thinking, 'Maybe I've been too quick to judge these sumbucks, maybe this'll be the one to change my mind.' But then the kid looks me right in the eye and says, 'Oh, there is one thing. I can't work on Sundays. It's against my religion.' I couldn't help it. I laughed in his face. I said, 'Son, the way I see it is this. God made these animals, and they have to eat, Sunday or no Sunday. You think Noah took Sunday off, and just let all the animals on the Ark starve to death? I don't think so. The way I see it, the feedlot *is* our church, and feeding these cattle is our way of praising God, and if we do a good enough job, maybe we'll get to heaven like all good Christians do in the end.' And having said that, I kicked that snotty-nosed little punk out of my office and went on back to work."

Joaquin was a roofer when he started working for Bill. He knew nothing about cattle and had never ridden a horse in his life. But unlike the saddle bums who sometimes showed up at the scale house looking for a day's or a week's work, he had no preconceived notions about how to do the job. If Bill told him to look the same direction every time he rode pens, so that the cattle flowed past him precisely the same way, day in and day out, that's exactly what Joaquin did. He had no bad habits as a horseman, because Bill had taught him everything he knew, and Bill himself had no bad habits. As for the long hours, low pay, and paltry benefits—the same was true of roofing, beef packing, and a dozen other jobs, none of which featured the added benefit of being able to perform at least some of the work from the back of a horse.

There's a curious, full-circle quality to this. Fifty years before there was a cattle industry in Texas or Kansas, Spanish-speaking vaqueros in California had already set the tone and established the equipment, techniques, and much of the vocabulary used in the work. The cowboy's distinctive hat, boots, spurs, and saddle are all of Spanish origin, as are many cowboy words, such as *lariat* (from *la reata*), *dally* (*dar la vuelta*), *chaps* (*chaparreras*), *buckaroo* (*vaquero*), and so on. Even the American quarter horse, the mount of choice among American cowboys for more than a century, can be traced in part to horses brought to the New World from Spain in the fifteenth century. Like the men who rode them, these horses were small but hardy, requiring little in the way of food or water to do a notoriously tough job.

Yet there is a strange, otherworldly quality to all of this, too. How many Americans would guess that nine out of ten people working in the feedlot and beef packing industries in places such as southwestern Kansas are recent arrivals from Mexico, many of them without documentation? Almost everyone in Kansas knows, of course. But America is not Kansas. Not yet, anyway.

By 10:30 in the morning, we had finished implanting, vaccinating, and tagging new arrivals at the feedlot. It was time to get back in the saddle to ride pens. This was the work I had imagined myself doing when I was first visited by the notion of spending a day working as a feedlot cowboy. However, the idea that I would be given pens of my own to ride turned out to be pure fantasy on my part. Riding pens in Bill's feedlot was precision work meant to be done according to a playbook I hadn't mastered. Rather than ride pens of my own, I had to tag along with Joaquin and try to get a feel for the work that way. Even this broke one of Bill's cardinal rules—the one against cowboys "buddying up" and riding pens together, which according to Bill only led to sloppy decision making and a lack of concentration. "Saddle bums love to ride pens together," Bill liked to say, "and that's just one of the reasons why they suck at their jobs and usually do more harm than good. Instead of eyeballing a cow and making a decision, they sit there on their horses and *talk* about it. 'Does she look bloated to you? No? Well, maybe you're right' . . . Idiots!"

We started on the east side of the feed yard, taking the pens one at a time, riding quietly in, closing the gate behind us, and then inspecting each animal as it flowed past us from right to left, looking for sluggishness, slowness to get up, runny noses or eyes, and the tell-tale signs of bloat or acidosis, a condition caused by a too-rapid or overconsumption of grain.

The cattle in the first few pens were recent arrivals—fast, squirrelly animals that scampered out of our way as soon as we entered their pen. You had to be slow and steady around these cattle, so as not to spook or stress them.

"See the little black one?" Joaquin asked in a quiet voice, nodding at an undersized calf that seemed to want to hide from us, attaching itself to a bigger calf as if to its mother. "How slow he's moving? We'll pull him out."

The next time the cattle flowed past us, Joaquin cut the black calf out of the herd and held him against the fence while the rest of the herd flowed to the opposite end of the pen. Then, as Joaquin trotted over to open a gate to the alley, Cuba and I held the calf there, the horse coming to life beneath me, matching every move and fake the calf threw at him, until finally the calf had been delivered through the gate and into the alley.

"Nice," Joaquin said, nodding at Cuba. "How much you want for him?"

"Sorry," I said. "He's my brother Dave's horse. Not for sale."

"Bill says he picked the horse out himself at an auction. But then he was ruined. Too much roping."

"Yes, I know all about that."

The man shrugged broadly. "He look good to me, though. We'll pick up little blackie on our way back."

The cattle in the next pen looked remarkably different from the yearlings we had just left. These were "finished" cattle, nearing the end of their stay at the feedlot. Many were lying down when we rode into their pen, and they were slow to get to their feet. Several times I had to ride almost on top of a cow to get it to move, and even then it was with the slow, stiff-leggedness of the morbidly obese.

"What about that one?" I asked Joaquin, nodding at an enormous black cow that waddled out of our way with great deliberateness. "Anything wrong with him?"

"No, just fat," Joaquin said.

But fat did not begin to describe this cow. He looked as if someone had inserted an air hose beneath his hide and inflated him to his present, blimp-like proportions. There was something awful, yet awe-inspiring, too, about this enormous beast. Looking at him was like looking at a champion bodybuilder or a blue-ribbon steer. He was a freak, to be sure, but he was also the product of an entire industry's striving for a certain kind of perfection. Not just ranchers and cowboys but men and women in lab coats with advanced degrees from the best universities in the land had produced him. Wash the mud off his hide and give him a quick shampoo, and he'd be a good bet to win the fair.

In another pen, we came upon a similarly fat cow, only this one had what looked to be a basketball sticking out of its left side. "Is that one just fat, too?" I asked.

"No, she bloated," Joaquin said, circling the cow quietly. "We put her in the alley with the little black one."

As the morning wore on, Joaquin and I worked our way through a line of pens running parallel to those being ridden by Jose, Sergio, and Jaime. The sun was fully out now, and the cowboys had put away their feed caps and donned wide-brimmed straw hats. This was the longest and most important part of the day we would spend on horseback, and there was a pleasure in the work that for me stood in direct contrast to the feet-bound work of processing. Every half hour or so, we would stop at a concrete water trough in the pen we were working and let our horses take a long drink. I would sit up straight in my saddle and look off in the distance, often catching sight of another pen rider silhouetted against the horizon. It was the same iconic scene my son, Jake, and I had spied out the window on our way west from Kansas City. Now, as then, there was something oddly grand about it. Despite the degradation of our surroundings, some small part of the romance of cowboy life continued to live on here.

Halfway through our assigned pens, I decided it was time for me to contribute something to the work we were doing. If I couldn't be trusted to determine which cattle to pull, at least I could relieve Joaquin of the necessity of opening and shutting all those gates.

The top of a rectangular feedlot gate is four and a half feet off the ground, or about as high as the average horse's shoulder. Set on hinges and made of two-inch steel pipe, the gate swings in or out and is secured by an iron slip-rod set on a forty-five-degree angle. Hurrying ahead of Joaquin, I rode right up to the first gate we came to, held Cuba's right side in check with my spur, and reached down with my left hand to push the gate open wide enough for Joaquin and his horse to pass through. After he had done so, I side-passed Cuba again, pushing the gate in front of us, and dropped the slip-rod, closing it. Soon I was riding ahead to open and shut every gate we came to. Maybe the action wasn't as fluid or pretty as when Joaquin did it, but it was passable work, and I felt good doing it.

Then we came upon a corner gate set on the edge of a slippery embankment with a pool of quicksand-like mud at the base of it. This was a different kind of challenge, and Cuba responded to it by being even more keyed-up and impatient than usual. Still I managed to hold him on the embankment while I pushed the gate open before me and we stepped through. However, as I spun the horse's hindquarters around, the gate slipped from my hand and swung back into the alley with a rush, narrowing missing Joaquin and his horse.

"Shit, sorry," I said. "Let me get it."

But by then Joaquin already had the gate in his hand. "Open it this way, toward you," he said, demonstrating. "It's easier that way."

"Thanks," I said, feeling the red rise up from my neck and into my ears. As crazy and unrealistic as the desire was, I really did want to do the job on the same level as Joaquin and the others. No matter how many gates I flubbed or ear tags I dropped on the floor, the desire remained. Why? What accounted for it? I couldn't say. All I knew was that it was there inside me like some ancient and useless mutation.

We pulled a dozen sick cattle during the two hours we spent riding pens that day. Only one cow was a case of acidosis. The rest were pulled for symptoms ranging from lethargy to a runny nose. These we pushed as a single herd up the main alley of the feedlot to a holding pen behind the "hospital," or doctoring barn, where Bill awaited us.

"This is the third time in the hospital for that bloat," he observed, looking over the cattle we had pulled. It was clear from watching him that every fiber in Bill's body was engaged by his work. After thirty-five years working in various feedlots, the man could be expected to have grown sick of it by now. But we all tend to gravitate toward work we're good at, and Bill's special talent was keeping animals alive—right up to the moment they were shipped to the slaughterhouse to die.

We ate lunch in a hamburger joint/bowling alley in the middle of Scott City. "What do you think of my crew?" Bill asked, after our order was in.

"They're good," I said.

"Goddamn right they are," he said with a smile and a nod. "I put that team together myself, trained every last one of them. They're *cross-trained*. Every cowboy on the crew can drive a feed truck, and the feed truck drivers, in a pinch, can ride pens. Joaquin is the captain of the team. They're all accountable to him, and he's accountable to me. They're related, too. Sergio is Jose's little brother. Did you happen to notice that?"

"No, I didn't," I said.

Bill nodded again. "I think the world of those boys, I really do. I'd do anything for them. Of course, if they started screwing up, I'd fire them, too. You have to be that way, or they'll walk all over you."

For the next forty-five minutes, while I slammed a cheeseburger and onion rings and three Diet Cokes, Bill regaled me with stories from his career as a "fixer" of feedlots.

"You get some guy who doesn't know his head from his ass running one of these places, and he goes and hires a bunch of idiots, thieves, and other degenerates, and pretty soon the inmates are running the asylum and the cattle are standing there in their own muck, sick and starving to death. Things get bad enough, the phone starts ringing. 'Homer, can you *please* come clean up this terrible mess we've made out here?' What can I say? It's what I do."

"Do you ever get a hankering to work for one of the really big outfits?" I asked. "A hundred thousand head? Bigger?"

"Hell, no. Those aren't feedlots. They're disasters waiting to happen. They don't even use horses in those yards. They fly over the pens in helicopters, look out the windows of pickups, shit like that. It's all a numbers game to them. Sorry, but I'm not built that way."

I finished my cheeseburger and sat there with a wide grin on my face.

"What?" Bill asked.

"You're coaching," I said, having saved up the insight for just this moment. "It's not football, but you still treat it like a game. Maybe that's why it's still fun for you."

"You know what?" Bill said, smiling broadly. "You're right about that. And I'll tell you something else, too. If we got to play in *games*, if feedlot cowboying was a competitive enterprise, we'd kick the ass of any other feedlot crew in the state, bar none. I'm telling you, boy. We'd run them right off the field."

"What about me?" I asked. "Would I make it off the bench?"

The question took Bill by surprise. "Well, maybe. After a while," he said with all the diplomacy he could muster.

The hospital was a cement-floored building the size of a large suburban garage. A high-sided crowd alley and squeeze chute similar to the one in the processing barn dominated the floor plan, which included a small room for storing veterinary supplies and a computer terminal for checking animal health records. One by one, each of the animals we had pulled that morning, as well as those that remained in the hospital from the day before, were driven up the alley and into the squeeze chute, where Sergio, wearing surgical gloves, inserted an anal thermometer and Jose read the animal's tag number to Bill, who entered it into the computer.

JOSE: One oh eight five four.

BILL: Five four?

JOSE: Yes, five four.

BILL: Temp?

SERGIO: One oh three.

BILL: A little hot. Let's give this little cow ten units of Draxxin and keep him here another day.

Upon hearing this, Sergio drew the dose into a syringe and gave the cow an injection in the side of its neck, just above the shoulder. Then as Bill updated the cow's medical chart, Jose released the animal from the squeeze chute, and Sergio ran in the next cow in line.

Although neither Jose nor Sergio spoke much English, they had no trouble understanding Bill's instructions to them. Once, hearing Bill call for forty-four cc's of a particular drug and seeing Sergio draw only twenty-two, I pointed out the discrepancy to him, whereupon Sergio showed me that the syringe held only thirty cc's. "I draw two times twenty-two," he explained. After that, I kept my mouth shut and watched.

When the bloated cow was run into the chute, Bill sighed and said, "She's a chronic. Probably she won't make it, but you never know."

Jose ran a length of flexible hose down the cow's throat and into its stomach while Bill and I pushed on the basketball-sized bloat on the cow's left side, causing the gas collected there to make a sharp hissing sound as it escaped through the hose.

"All right, I think that's it," Bill said.

Hearing this, Sergio patted the animal's head with something like affection, then opened the chute, releasing her into the outer corral, where Jaime stood ready to load her into a trailer for transport back to the pen from which she had been pulled a few hours before.

We finished doctoring sick cattle a little after 3:30 p.m., exactly twelve hours after I had gotten out of bed that morning. By then I was tired enough that I could have lain down on the concrete floor of the processing barn and fallen straight to sleep. Instead, we mounted back up (by now I was on Doc, my second horse of the day) and rode out into the feedlot to bring in a group of seventy-five heifers that had arrived earlier in the day. By the time we finished processing this last group and were driving them back to their home pen on the far side of the feedlot, it was after 6:00.

As we made our way back to the barn at the end of that long day, the cowboys chatted amiably in Spanish, and Joaquin performed a kind of jig on his horse, side-passing him down the middle of the alley. Watching this dance, it struck me that despite the long hours and grueling nature of the work, feedlot cowboying, at least the way it was practiced at Bill's feedlot, was still one of the few jobs left in America that a man got to do from horseback. You couldn't say that about a factory job or an office job, and God knows you couldn't say it about working in a beef packing plant. This element was what saved the job from mere drudgery, elevating it to a status just this side of myth.

Still, none of this was enough to make me want to come back and do it all over again the next day, and I told Bill as much as I was loading Cuba and Doc into the trailer for the hour and a half ride back to the ranch.

"I figured as much," Bill said, sucking on a toothpick he had saved from lunch. "I'll be here, though, and so will Joaquin and Jose and the rest. After all, cattle have to eat, even on Sunday."

I stopped to consider this. There was more to Bill's attitude, I saw now, than braggadocio and an out-of-control work ethic.

"You really do love it, don't you?" I asked. "The work, the smell, the endless, repetitive nature of the job. 'A cowboy's work is never done.' All that shit."

"Well, love's a strong word," Bill demurred, sucking at the toothpick. "But sure. I love it. Why the hell not?"

Only a cowboy could.

How to Ride a Bronc

> Bronc riding isn't one of them half-hearted-effort deals.
>
> —Dan Etbauer

Growing up around horses and ranch people does not guarantee that one will develop an interest in rodeo, any more than growing up around snow guarantees an interest in skiing. However, having this background does at least admit the *possibility* of such an interest taking root; and should the interest happen to grow, metastasizing to the point at which others begin to doubt one's mental equilibrium, well, then, at least one knows where to go to find people capable of aiding and abetting one in the craziness.

"Am I nuts or what?" I asked Kent Crouch, the Dodge City Community College rodeo coach, a man I knew only through e-mail messages and long-distance phone conversations.

"Heck, no," Crouch said in his characteristic nasal twang—the same twang that I could still summon if the need or the desire arose. "The way I look at it, if a guy gets to thinking he wants to ride broncs, then that's probably something he ought to look into. Of course," he added with a laugh, "it would've been a whole lot better if you'd had this idea *twenty-five years ago . . .*"

"No doubt," I said, laughing myself.

It was the week after the Fourth of July. The Dodge City Roundup, my hometown's annual, week-long rodeo, was a little more than ten days away. For the past couple of days, I'd been running the idea of a bronc-riding adventure past various people

I knew in Dodge City, and to my amazement, they all seemed to like the idea. "I don't see a problem so long as you sign a release," a media relations person with the Roundup said to me.

"Really?" I said, incredulous.

"Sure," the woman answered, sounding a little bored now. "Why not?"

The response in Indianapolis had been very different.

"Have you LOST YOUR FUCKING MIND?" a colleague asked. "You're a forty-something university professor. You've got no business riding broncs."

"Billy Etbauer is forty-six," I countered.

"*Who?*"

"Billy Etbauer. The greatest saddle bronc rider in the world."

"My God, you're serious, aren't you? Listen to me. *Don't do it!* Come to your senses before it's too late!"

But as far as I was concerned, it already was too late. A part of me was already on that bronc, waiting for the chute to fly open and whatever happened after that to catapult me into some new, more passionate existence.

At dinner the night I talked to Crouch, my wife, Alyssa, sat wordlessly, head in her hands, while I ticked off some of the factors that made bronc riding a "safer option" than bull riding. "First of all, a bronc won't come after you when you're bucked off, the way a bull will," I began.

"Please," Alyssa said, holding up a hand to stop me. "The less I know about this, the better off I'm going to be. I need just one thing from you right now, and that's a promise you'll buy more life insurance before you leave."

"Life insurance!" I laughed. "You're kidding, right?"

"Do I *look* like I'm kidding?" she responded.

As a kid growing up in western Kansas, I never paid much attention to rodeo. It was just another of my hometown's hick pastimes, of which there were too many to count. I didn't attend my first Roundup until I was fifteen or sixteen years old, and even then it was just to hang out with my friends and sneak beer, the entire ragtag bunch of us dressed in concert T-shirts and tennis shoes. We understood that rodeo traced its roots to the days when Dodge was the unquestioned Queen of the Cowtowns and that the Roundup, held each year the week after Cheyenne Frontier Days, was one of the largest and richest rodeos on the professional circuit. However, none of this moved us very much. Rodeo to us was a hokey, hodgepodge affair—a track meet crossed with a circus, with a few embarrassing barnyard skits tossed in for good measure. It was hick stuff. If not for the easy access to beer, we wouldn't have ventured out to the rodeo grounds at all.

Only later, as an adult returning to Dodge to visit family and friends, did I begin to sit in the grandstands and actually watch rodeo. Even then, much of it bored me to tears. There was no overarching narrative tension in rodeo that I could discern—no score to follow or home team to root for, no innings or clock to mark time, no subplot pitting offense against defense, no underdog squaring off against a heavy favorite, and so on. Instead there was a parade of disparate events held loosely together by the narrating voice of the rodeo announcer, an overbearing, countrified figure who interpreted the action, told cornball jokes, and kept up a running banter with the clowns and judges.

There was, however, one aspect of rodeo that never failed to hold my attention, and that was the rough stock events of bareback, saddle bronc, and bull riding. If rodeo as a whole was a mishmash lacking tension, in the rough stock events there was action and drama aplenty. Indeed, a different story unfolded each time the gate to a bucking chute flew open. Would the rider make it to eight seconds or not? And if not, what fate awaited him once he was bucked off? Would he get a hand hung up in his rigging? A boot caught in a stirrup? Would he be stomped, dragged across the arena like a rag doll, gored to death? Unlike the contestants in the timed events, who competed against each other and a clock, the rough stock riders were caught up in an epic struggle pitting man against beast, maybe even man against nature itself. The spectators in the stands, as well as those leaning against the arena fence to get a closer look at the action, sensed this. Each time the gate opened on a new ride, you could hear the crowd suck in a collective breath that would not be released until the ride ran its course five or ten seconds later. Even then, the drama didn't dissipate so much as it was held in abeyance until the next chute was opened, and then the next.

From the first, I was always most drawn to the saddle bronc event. There was something about it that just seemed more authentic, more "real" to me. Maybe this was because I had grown up around saddle horses and had been bucked off more than a few. Each time it happened, there was always that same gathering of energy, followed by the telltale arching of the back, the first powerful kick of the hind legs, and that *moment,* lightning quick yet clear as a bell, when you had to decide whether you were going to bail off the horse or try to ride the thing out. For weeks or even months after one of these episodes, that moment would live on in the mind. Remembering, I would smile, shake my head, maybe even laugh aloud. *You know,* I would sometimes think, *in a weird way, the whole thing was kind of fun.*

It was while in the throes of such remembering that I found myself typing the words "saddle bronc riding highlights" into YouTube last summer. The clip that popped up, posted by a user named rwillie22 and set to the tune of AC/DC's "Hell's Bells," instantly lit a fire deep inside me. I played the clip over and over, the ominous opening notes of the song becoming wedded in my mind with the violent rhythms of bronc riding. That was when the idea began to take shape in my mind.

What the hell, I began to think.

I pulled into Dodge City the Sunday before the Roundup to find the place decked out in all its prerodeo glory. Half the bars and restaurants on Wyatt Earp Boulevard sported vinyl signs reading WELCOME RODEO FANS. The parking lot in front of Wal-Mart was full of diesel pickups pulling six- and eight-horse trailers. The motels and even the campgrounds had their neon NO VACANCY lights on.

In the days leading up to my arrival in Dodge, I'd done everything I could to get ready to ride broncs short of actually riding one. I read books on rodeo and visited websites devoted to its finer points. I ordered a DVD, *Get the Winning Edge: Saddle Bronc Riding with the Etbauers,* and studied the thing as if Billy Etbauer himself were going to show up on my doorstep and quiz me on it. I performed Internet searches into what kind of boots and chaps to wear, then dropped $218 on a pair of slick-bottomed Olathes (so as not to get hung up in a stirrup) and $235 on some leather batwing chaps (so as to better grip the swells of the saddle). I found a used bronc saddle to borrow—not an easy thing in the middle of rodeo season— and arranged to pick it up from its owner, Lyle Sankey of the Sankey Rodeo Company, on my way west. Most importantly, I called Kent Crouch at the community college and got him to take me on as a student.

On late Tuesday afternoon, I met up with Crouch and my friend Shane Bangerter, a Dodge City lawyer who seemed to understand what I was after better than most, at the dirt-floored pole barn that houses the community college's rodeo program. It was the tail end of a hot day, every bit of 95 degrees, and I found Crouch, a lean, sunburned man in a straw cowboy hat and creased Wranglers, standing in the shade of the barn talking to someone on a cell phone. As I came up, he covered the phone with his free hand and called out in a loud voice, "I talked to the folks out at Roundup this afternoon, and there ain't no way in hell we're getting you on a horse out there."

"What?" I said, feeling as if I'd been punched in the gut. "I talked to them last week. They said it was no problem."

"That was last week," Crouch said. "It's busier than hell out there, and they just don't have time for the kind of shenanigans we got planned."

I stood there, shaking my head with disbelief.

"Hell, quit looking so glum," Crouch said after a minute. "I've got a guy on the line here you need to talk to." And with that, he held out the cell phone to me to take.

"Hello?" I said.

"I hear you're a man who wants to ride broncs," came a twangy voice that sounded eerily familiar.

"I am," I said. "Can you help me out?"

"Son, you better believe I can . . ."

The caller turned out to be Tyrone Crouch, a cousin of Kent's who ran a rodeo at the Wichita County Fair in Leoti, two hours west of Dodge City. Not only was there a spot open in the rodeo for me to ride, but Tyrone seemed to think that the farmers and ranchers of Leoti would enjoy seeing a middle-aged college professor catapulted into the air by a twelve-hundred-pound bronc. "Call us crazy, but we kind of like that sort of thing," he said. "How does Friday night suit you?"

"Perfect," I answered, feeling a rush of adrenaline coming on.

"Well, then," Tyrone said, "it looks to me like you've got yourself a date with a bronc."

I folded the phone and handed it back to Crouch.

"Are we in business?" Shane asked.

I nodded, smiling from ear to ear.

We strapped my bronc saddle onto one of the college's hand-operated bucking machines, a device that looked something like a padded thirty-gallon barrel mounted longways onto a teeter-totter. "Now, the first thing you've got to understand," Crouch said, going into teacher mode, "is that there ain't no way in hell we're gonna make this thing feel like a real bucking horse. That just ain't possible. All we can do is approximate a couple of positions you'll find yourself in, and then go over what your plan ought to be when the chute gate flies open and all hell breaks loose."

"Fine," I said. "Let's do it."

For the next twenty minutes, while Crouch shouted instructions and Shane teeter-tottered the machine as hard as he could, I tried to get a feel for the one-two rhythm of bronc riding. When the bronc set its front feet in the dirt and kicked, I was to stay back in the saddle, turn out my toes, and grab hold of the horse's shoulders with my spurs. On the next beat, when the horse exploded upward off its hind legs, I was to spur hard from his shoulders to the back of my saddle, "lifting" all the while on the thick, grass rein, and using my free hand as a kind of counter balance.

"Coil and reach," Crouch called out. "Coil and reach. Coil and reach . . ."

To my surprise, I had no trouble staying in time with the mechanical horse. The hard part was getting my toes turned out far enough to set my spurs in the horse's neck. No matter how hard I tried, I just couldn't get my feet to conform to that exaggerated "duck walk" position. I lacked the flexibility in my ankles, knees, and hips.

"I wouldn't worry too much about that," Crouch said after watching me struggle. "They say them South Dakota boys start working on their spur out when they're six or seven years old, so it's not like you're gonna pick it up in a couple of days. Besides, when that gate flies open, you'll have time to think about one or two things max, and it won't be how pretty your feet look."

I nodded, wiping sweat from my brow, then posed the question that had been forming in my head for days. "Do you think I've got a chance in hell of making the whistle?"

"Hey, *you're* the only sumbitch in the world who can answer that question." Crouch shrugged dramatically. "The only thing I can tell you is to stay back in your saddle, lift on your rein, and try your goddamn guts out. The way this deal is shaking out, you're only going to get one shot at riding that horse, and when it's all said and done, you don't want to have any regrets in the effort department. Know what I mean?"

"I know exactly what you mean." I climbed down from the bucking machine to shake Crouch's hand. "I just wish I could get on a bronc right now. All this waiting is killing me."

"Welcome to rodeo," Crouch said. "Eight seconds of action packed into a day and a half of driving and standing around. It's awful fun, though. You'll see."

Wednesday was Family Night at the Dodge City Roundup. Six thousand people, give or take, poured into the spectators' side of the rodeo grounds to enjoy fireworks, free hamburgers, and the first of five consecutive nights of rodeo action. An atmosphere something like a carnival or a small state fair prevailed, as people milled about gabbing and drinking beer. The vibe on the contestants' side, however, could not have been more different. Here all was business. A crew from a local TV station interviewed a barrel racer, while, ten feet away, a roper loped his horse around the plowed-up practice arena, eyes narrowed in concentration. In the enclosed space behind the bucking chutes, rough stock riders checked their gear, stretched, and got taped up, all of these preparations done with the same methodical precision you might see in an NFL locker room. As for the rodeo itself, the riders paid little attention to it beyond noting where their event fell in the overall program.

An hour before they were scheduled to ride, the saddle bronc riders laid their saddles in the dirt and went through an elaborate preride ritual that included practicing their spur out— that exaggerated duck-walk positioning of the feet and spurs I still hadn't mastered—and working rosin into their chaps and the swells of their saddles. Sitting in his saddle in the dirt, a rider would lift the pommel off the ground with his left hand, hold it aloft for a second, and then drop it, digging at the air before him with his spurs, while at the same time pretending to lift with his rein hand. Over and over, as many as fifteen or twenty times, riders would repeat this same series of motions. It was some species of psycho-cybernetics, what Dan Etbauer, in *Get the Winning Edge*, called "riding the horse in your head." Only when each motion felt perfectly natural would a cowboy kick out of his stirrups, loosen his chaps, and wait for his horse to be rolled into the narrow alleys that led to the bucking chutes.

When the time to ride drew nearer still, a new set of preparations took place, as one by one each rider saddled and haltered
his horse, measured for where he would hold his rein, and pulled
the front cinch on the saddle tight. That done, the rider would
climb onto the chute above his horse and go through the last details of his routine, which often included a short prayer punctu-
ated by a hat-off, eyes-closed Sign of the Cross. By then the stock
contractor had stopped by to make sure everything was ready to
go. When the rider's turn finally arrived, three or four rodeo offi-
cials, including judges and those responsible for opening the gate
and pulling the horse's flank strap tight, would converge on the
chute. Wasting no time, yet not hurrying either, the rider would
climb into his saddle, get his feet set in the stirrups, tuck his chin
against his chest, and call for the gate to be opened.

What happened next was an explosion, a colossal gathering together and expending of energy, as if rider and horse had
been flung into the arena by some huge, invisible hand. A G-
force-inducing, whiplash effect was created, as the rider's legs
and hips shot forward into the arena along with the horse, while
his head and free arm remained momentarily behind, until they
too were sucked into the maelstrom of the ride.

Ka-BOOM!
Whoooooooooooooooooooooooosh!

I loved that moment. The rest of the ride was exciting, too,
of course. But that moment of stasis giving way to explosion
was what really drew me in. The power and beauty of it was
intoxicating. Each night while I drove home from the Roundup,
a kind of composite version of the moment would stay with
me. I'd go to sleep thinking about it, and when I woke the next
morning, there it still would be, waiting for me.

What will it be like to experience that? I'd wonder.

Friday afternoon, I threw my bronc saddle into the back of
Shane's Corvette, and we headed west across the plains toward
Garden City. We had planned to fly to Leoti in Shane's and my
brother's four-seater Beechcraft, but the sky in that direction

had turned into a tower of billowing, steel-gray clouds, and we decided to take the highway instead.

"Think it's gonna rain?" I asked.

"Maybe," Shane said. "The thing is, a rodeo goes on no matter what the weather is doing. If I were you, I'd get ready to get wet."

We fell silent a moment, then I asked, "What's the most fun thing you've ever done in your life?"

"Probably taking the green flag in the middle of a pack of sprint cars," Shane said. "How about you?"

"Football. Seeing the opening kickoff go up into the lights above the field, and knowing I was going to be the one to haul it down and take off running."

"I remember that," Shane said, nodding, as that ominous bank of black clouds continued to build in the west.

We pulled into the Wichita Country Fairgrounds a little before seven to find Tyrone Crouch—dressed, like everyone else, in a long-sleeved shirt and Wranglers—in the thick of pre-rodeo preparations. "Did you bring your slicker?" Tyrone asked me.

"Shane's got one," I said.

"Any butterflies?"

"A few. Impatient to get going, more than anything."

"Uh-huh." Tyrone nodded in a knowing way. "Well, you won't have to wait much longer. We'll get going in about forty-five minutes or so."

Everything about the rodeo at Leoti, from the grandstands to the announcer's stand to the pens holding the livestock, was on a smaller scale than in Dodge City. Still, it was exciting to pass through the area behind the bucking chutes and see the horses and bulls waiting in their pens. I stood watching a moment as they milled and wheeled about. I tried to guess which horse would be mine. Would it be the stocky roan with the wild eyes? The sorrel with the blond mane? The big bay that stood off by itself, as though it had been through all of this too many times to care?

I ate a cheeseburger with Shane, then fetched my saddle from the Corvette. By the time I got back, the bareback riders were already deep into their preride rituals. After dropping my gear in the dirt, I put on my chaps and spurs and began to rub rosin into the swells of my saddle. While I was at this, the stock contractor, the man responsible for providing the rodeo with a string of bulls and bucking horses, stopped by the bucking chutes, and I took the opportunity to ask what horse I'd be riding. "That big sorrel back there," he said, nodding toward a huge, light brown horse with a blond mane.

"What can you tell me about him?" I asked.

"He's a good one, don't you worry," the contractor said with that same amused gleam in his eye Tyrone had shown me earlier. "Older horse, not a lot of drop, but he'll buck for you. I think you'll like him a lot."

The bareback and saddle bronc horses were rolled into their chutes. One by one the riders climbed over the top rail and were launched into the arena like jets catapulted off the deck of an aircraft carrier. I sat in my bronc saddle, eyes closed, riding the big sorrel "in my head." Nod. Gate flies open. Spur out. Lift. Find a rhythm. Stay back in the saddle . . .

Then the wind picked up, and the thunder I'd been hearing for the past half hour began to get more raucous. To the south and west, sheet lightning ripped across a black sky.

"It's fixing to rain," one of the other riders said.

No sooner had this been announced than a couple of fat raindrops hit the brim of my hat.

"Well, shit," another rider said.

The stock contractor began to have trouble loading the horses. With all the lightning and wind, they wanted no part of the narrow alley leading up to the chutes. Finally Shane went back to help him. Three times they brought the big sorrel up the narrow alley behind the ranch broncs, and each time one of the horses in front of him balked, backing out of the alley, and the whole thing had to be done over. *If they could just load my horse in front of the others,* I thought. But I knew that wasn't going to happen. There was a preestablished order to the way things were supposed to come off, and nobody was going to change that just to suit me.

Finally, after the third unsuccessful attempt to load the horses, the stock contractor stood off to the side and let them stampede past him into the large holding pen far behind the bucking chutes.

"Sorry, fellas," he said to those of us who were waiting to ride. "They're just too riled up. We're gonna have to come back to you later on."

"When?" one of the other riders asked.

"After the bull riding."

A wave of disappointment washed over me. Bull riding was the final event of the evening, after the barrel racing and a couple of roping events. Nobody hung around a rodeo after the bull riding was over. It was garbage time—"slack," as they called it. Would there even be a rodeo, properly speaking, by the time I got to ride? *If* I got to ride?

Then the sky opened up and it began to hail. In a matter of seconds, the ground was covered with marble-sized hunks of ice. Holding my hat on my head, I grabbed my saddle and other gear and sought shelter under the announcer's stand. Eight or nine riders joined me there, all of us crammed together in a space no bigger than an elevator. Meanwhile, in the pens behind us, the horses roiled about in a futile attempt to evade the hail—this in contrast to the stoical bulls, who merely lowered their heads and took it where they stood.

"Ain't this a pretty sight?" one of the bull riders, a kid of nineteen or twenty, asked.

"It'll blow over in a minute," another rider predicted.

"Yeah, and the arena will be soup," a third said.

"I don't give a shit so long as I get to ride," the first rider said to no one in particular. I saw now that he had his right arm in a sling. His battered Stetson was almost completely soaked through with water. It occurred to me then that getting a late start on my rodeo career might actually be safer than having gotten an early start.

"What happened to your arm?" I asked.

"Nothing wrong with my arm," the kid answered. "It's my shoulder that hurts. I dislocated it at a rodeo over in Colorado on Tuesday night."

"And you're riding anyway?"

"What the hell else have I got to do?" he asked, laughing.

Then, as abruptly as it had begun, the hail stopped, and the announcer came on the PA system to call the beginning of the calf roping.

Forty minutes later, the space behind the bucking chutes had regained its energy and sense of purpose. The sky overhead was black and calm, and the bull riders were slapping themselves in the face, getting ready to ride. I pulled on my chaps and spurs, scraped the old rosin off my saddle with a wire brush, and applied new. Dropping into my saddle, I slipped my feet into the oxbow stirrups and practiced my spur out.

Then the stock contractor loaded my horse along with the others that were left to go. I looked the animal over from top to bottom, seeing him as if for the first time. He was a magnificent beast—every bit of sixteen hands, tall and thick through the neck, shoulders, and haunches in the manner of a Budweiser Clydesdale. How many cowboys had he launched into the air? How many had he kicked, stepped on, or dragged in the dirt behind him? Did this work please him, or was he just waiting to get it over with so he could go back to his stall in the contractor's trailer and fall asleep standing up?

With the help of the stock contractor and a couple of riders who had stayed behind to see me ride, I got the horse saddled, then measured for the spot where I would hold the rein, marking it with a strand of blond mane hair. That done, I climbed up on top of the chute and waited.

"Are you ready?" one of the cowboys asked.

"I guess we're about to find out," I said.

"No, we're not about to *find out*," came a voice below me. Looking down, I saw the twenty-year-old kid who had just won the bull riding despite having to take his arm out of a sling to do it. "And you're not *guessing* about anything, either. You're gonna *ride* that son of a bitch. End of story."

"You're right," I said, gritting my teeth. "I'm gonna ride him."

The stock contractor pulled the front cinch tight, and I stepped over the top of the chute.

"Try like hell," another rider said. "No quit."

I climbed into the saddle and eased my boots into the stirrups, first my right foot, then my left. Then I checked my rein one last time and, feeling a sudden calm come over me, tucked my chin into my chest and nodded for the gate.

"Let's go!"

The chute gate flew open—*Ka-BAM!*—and I spurred the horse out. He took one medium-sized jump, then took off across the arena, half bucking and half running. I stayed back in the saddle and lifted on the rein until it felt like my shoulder might pop out of its socket. One—two—three jumps, and I was still with him, still deep in the saddle and in rhythm with the horse. *By God, I'm gonna make it,* I thought. *I'm halfway to the whistle right now . . .*

Then the horse reached the middle of the arena, ducked his head, and stopped hard on his front feet, and in that instant, all of the balance and rhythm I'd achieved disappeared. My butt came high out of the saddle, and when I tried to pull myself back down again, it was only to meet the horse on his next, bigger jump. I was out of rhythm. My tailbone crashed into the seat of the saddle, and I lost my left stirrup.

I knew I was in trouble. When the horse came down on his next jump, I was a goner for sure. Still I tried. I turned both feet out and lifted on the rein as hard as I could. The effort was bootless. When the horse ducked out to his left, I flew straight over his right shoulder.

In an instant, all of my efforts shifted from staying on the horse to getting off him in one piece. A single thought flashed through my mind: FOR GOD'S SAKE, DON'T GET HUNG UP! Kicking wildly with my right foot, I felt that stirrup fall free, and a second after that, I landed on my left hip in the plowed dirt of the arena. Perhaps a second and a half after that, I heard the arena horn go off, announcing what would have been the official end of my ride, had I made it that far.

Six seconds. On a horse that bolted as much as it bucked. That's how long I lasted. That's how good of a bronc rider I turned out to be.

And yet, as I made my way across the muddy arena, side-stepping the now-riderless horse as the pickup men herded him toward the gate that would return him to the pens behind the bucking chutes, all I could do was smile. Tipping my hat to the small crowd that remained in the stands, I smiled. Shaking first Tyrone's hand and then Shane's, I smiled some more.

"Well, you almost got her rode," Tyrone said.

"Yeah, almost," I said.

"Was it fun?"

"Are you kidding? You better believe it."

When I woke up the next morning—and for a month of mornings after that—there were parts of me that hurt so bad it took four Extra Strength Tylenol just to drag my ass out of bed. But even then, I was smiling.

Epilogue
THE CASINO

I had been hearing about the Boot Hill Casino and Resort for months before I finally worked up the enthusiasm to visit the place. Friends and relatives in Kansas would call or e-mail me with equal parts alarm and excitement, saying things like, "Oh my God, you've got to see this monstrosity!" or "If you're looking for something to write about, this is *it*."

But I would demur, telling them and myself that I had no interest in gambling, was "constitutionally incapable" of placing even a modest bet.

"You're interested in Dodge, aren't you?" one particularly adamant friend shot back at me. "Its history? Its future? Well, the casino is all that rolled into one neat package. Plus, it's really, really awful in ways you cannot begin to imagine."

Still, I procrastinated. I had visited casinos before, and they had always left me feeling wobbly-legged and trapped, like some doped-up rat in a science experiment. I had no desire to feel that way again, even if it was in service to my hometown.

I first heard about the casino when it was little more than a gash in the prairie with a few sticks hammered into the ground by a surveying crew. Later I was directed to a page on the *Daily Globe*'s website that featured a link to a grainy camera feed offering 24/7 views of the casino rising from the plains like some rough beast whose hour had come at last. Late one night, on the eve of a blizzard if I remember correctly, I accessed the feed and sat watching as snow swirled around naked girders and stranded earthmoving equipment and large swaths of congealed concrete. The sight depressed me. The land on which the casino prepared to rear its ugly head was less than a mile south of where my father's people had farmed since before the Great Depression. It was odd to think of something as gaudy and electrified as a casino rising up on what had always been, in my memory at least, a bindweed- and prairie dog–infested pasture. Hadn't I walked barefoot across that pasture on my way to swim at the American Legion pool? Hadn't I cursed the sticker patches I'd had to pick my way through, the wet cow patty I stepped in by accident? Hadn't I wished the whole kit-and-caboodle away? It seemed to me that I had, yet now I felt oddly protective of that very same pasture, as if it somehow represented all of the pristine forest and unspoiled natural grassland that had ever been raped in the name of "progress."

After the casino opened in December 2009, a story about its role in "revitalizing" the region's notoriously stagnant economy ran on CNN and was later archived on the network's website. From there, it bounced around Facebook and Twitter until it landed on my laptop in Indianapolis. The story told of how the civic leaders of Dodge City had used a penny sales tax increase to fund a slew of initiatives designed to transform the place from the smelly, slow-paced cowtown it had always been into an "entertainment mecca" based on Old West tourism. Stranger still, right smack in the middle of the glossy, highly produced video sat my cousin Kim Goodnight and several other people I recognized from Dodge City, all of them looking self-consciously "western" as well as highly pleased with themselves.

"It must be very strange," CNN reporter Tom Foreman observed before the assembled Dodge Citians, "to be sitting here, while the rest of the nation is in a recession, knowing that you're not."

After some self-satisfied chuckles, one of the Dodge Citians, a man identified as Jeff Highers, answered, "We took a vote in Dodge City and decided not to participate." More laughs. "That's what we did. We just decided that we would not participate in a recession."

How do you argue with that? I wondered as I watched the video a second and then a third time. Wasn't the economic strategy represented by the casino out of the same essential playbook Dodge City's founders had used a century and a half before, when they successfully lured the cattle business from railheads farther east and then proceeded to cash in on all the high-priced "entertainments" they were able to provide the young cowboys who rolled into town along with the herds? Wasn't it this aspect of the place, rather than its weather or natural beauty (such as it was!) that had attracted the likes of Bat Masterson, Doc Holliday, and Wyatt Earp to Dodge City in the first place?

The answer to all of these questions, needless to say, was a resounding *Yes.*

Yet I still found reasons to avoid the casino. I was in town for only a few days, I would tell myself; I was too busy reading and writing and riding horses. That was my true calling, not "bucking the tiger" on the inside of some air-conditioned nightmare. And so the closest I came to visiting the place was to follow the trail of new power lines across family land until they fed into the back of the casino complex, which from the distance of a mile looked like any other new cluster of buildings thrown up on previously undeveloped land—a suburban high school, say, or a megachurch. "Surely some revelation is at hand," I quoted to myself, gazing at the far-off buildings. "Surely the Second Coming is at hand. The Second Coming!"

Finally, however, the time came when even I, with my legendary powers of procrastination, could no longer withstand the pull of the casino.

It was the tail end of my most recent trip to Dodge City, and my wife, Alyssa, and I were enjoying a glass of wine with my seventy-eight-year-old mother when the subject of the casino came up, seemingly out of nowhere.

"I go out there sometimes with Sister Rosemary," my mother offered in passing. "The food's not great, but it sure is cheap."

"Sister Rosemary?" I asked. "Your friend, the *nun,* who goes on mission trips to Africa?"

"Sure," my mother answered defensively. "Why not? I mean, it's *her* money she gambles with . . ."

"That's it," I announced. "If nuns past retirement age have begun to frequent casinos, then I guess I can hold out no longer."

And so we drove west on Comanche Street, past the spot where the American Legion pool once stood, toward the halo of lights on the horizon thrown up by the casino.

"I don't want to stay long," Alyssa said. "I've spent too much time in casinos on business trips to Vegas. I've pretty much had it with them."

I nodded my assent, and she added a moment later, "Besides, Dodge City is not exactly Vegas, if you know what I mean."

"No," I said, feeling a tad put out by this comment. "I don't know what you mean. Why don't you tell me?"

"Ah, but I think you do," Alyssa said, refusing to rise to this bait.

Well, maybe I did know. But now that I had committed myself to the idea of gambling, my mind, as was its way, began to run wild with the possibilities. I imagined myself pushing open a pair of saloon-style wooden doors such as once hung at the entrance to the Long Branch Saloon. Once inside, I'd be hit in the face by the jangling sound of piano music and the voice of a tinhorn gambler calling out, "All right, boys, place your bets!" I saw myself walking, James Bond–like, up to a massive roulette wheel, where I'd smile at the croupier and place a single, crisp hundred-dollar bet on a number in the middle of the layout.

"A C-note on twenty-five red," I'd say.

And where would the ball land when the wheel stopped spinning?

Twenty-five—every time.

Driving into the parking lot, we were immediately confronted by the casino's jumbo video board, which featured a short clip of a cowboy riding a horse across the plains, followed by a series of casino come-on lines: HOTEL SHUTTLE! FREE VALET PARKING! $5.99 SEAFOOD BUFFET! Farther on, we rolled past row upon row of pickup trucks and minivans with license plates from Texas, Colorado, Oklahoma, Nebraska, and New Mexico, as well as most of the counties of central and western Kansas.

"Remember, just a short visit," Alyssa said as we got out of the Jeep. "I'm good for an hour, tops, and then I want to head back to the ranch."

"Come on," I teased her. "Live a little, why don't you. You want people to say that a *nun* is a higher roller than you are?"

"That wouldn't bother me at all," Alyssa said. "Like I told you, I've *done* casinos."

Pushing through the massive front doors, which were glass and nine or ten feet tall, we were instantly hit by a cacophony of bleeps and blips from the casino's five-hundred-plus slot machines. Cigarette smoke rose in plumes above the machines before being sucked into invisible air-cleaning equipment, while amid the clinking, clanking machines, retirees in track suits shuffled over the carpeted floor, most of them carrying cigarette packs in little leather purses.

At first glance, there was nothing Old West about any of it. We might have been on a "riverboat" sunk into the mud of the Mississippi west of St. Charles, or in some smoke-filled bingo parlor on a reservation in North Dakota, for all the difference it would have made.

A moment later, however, I saw that this was not exactly so. For above the casino floor rose a series of six-foot-high photomurals featuring nineteenth-century cowboys in various poses— around the campfire, branding cattle, sitting their horses amid a herd of Texas longhorns. I recognized the photos from books about Old Dodge City. Most had been taken south of the Arkansas River, where the herds that had been driven north from Texas were held until they could be loaded onto boxcars and shipped east to feed a nation suddenly ravenous for beef and all it represented. These teenaged cowboys, fresh from the trail and with two or three months' pay burning a hole in their pockets, had greased the wheel of early Dodge City's saloon/gambling/prostitution industry. Only now did the full of irony of all this strike me. For not one of these young men would be allowed inside today's casino, which held firm to a strict twenty-one-and-older policy and catered openly to a much older, more moneyed set. Indeed, today's slot-machine gambler was more likely to be female and somewhere between the ages of fifty and eighty than male and underage.

As I tried to communicate this irony to Alyssa over the din of the casino, we were approached out of nowhere by a mustachioed man in a period costume of stovepipe boots and a ten-gallon hat, a badge reading *Deputy Marshal* pinned to his vest. I hesitated briefly. Surely this was not a real . . . But no, there behind him, approaching us from the sea of slot machines, was a redheaded woman in the satiny garb of a nineteenth-century can-can dancer.

"Welcome to Boot Hill Casino and Resort," Marshal Dillon said, tipping his hat at Alyssa.

"We hope you enjoy your stay," Miss Kitty added, winking at me.

"Thank you," I answered for both of us.

"My God, it's like *Disneyland* or something," Alyssa observed after the pair had left us to greet other gamblers. "I'm going to the gift shop. What are you doing?"

"Getting a drink and heading to the roulette wheel. I mean to *gamble*, woman."

"Yeah, yeah," Alyssa said, already walking away. "I'll meet you there in a few."

Moving through the maze of slot machines, with their fanciful names such as "Stinkin Rich" and "Red Tiger" and "The Big Money"—not one of them, as far as I could see, Old West–related—I soon fetched up at the casino bar. The place was smaller than I had been expecting, perhaps twenty by forty feet, and crammed into that space were two poker tables where men in jeans and feed caps sat inspecting the hands dealt them by a pair of fat, uniformed dealers. Behind the bar, a greasy-haired man in his twenties failed to locate any Bookers, my preferred brand of bourbon. "Don't worry about it," I said. "Get me a double Jim Beam on the rocks instead."

"That I can do," he answered.

While I waited, my back against the bar, I did my best to nurture the illusion that I was in Old Dodge City, a thirsty cowboy just off the trail and looking for a good time. In my mind, the players at the two card tables looked me over with the same predatory knowingness that seasoned gamblers always displayed toward greenhorns. *Howdy, stranger. Care to sit in on a hand or two?* When the waiter brought me my eleven-dollar bourbon, I threw him a twenty and told him to keep the change.

"Thanks," he said without looking up.

Try as I might, the banks of flat screens displaying ESPN, ESPN2, CNN, and Fox News, as well as the piped-in sounds of John Mellencamp singing "Crumblin' Down," made the Old West illusion impossible to sustain. After knocking back half the bourbon, I headed across the casino floor to where the roulette table stood.

Along with faro and monte, roulette was a great favorite among gamblers of the Old West, and the reasons for this are not hard to find. Unlike more complicated games of chance, the rules of roulette are comparatively simple and clear: all one has to do to play is pick a spot on the layout and plunk some money down, and the spinning wheel with its little ball will take care of the rest.

Or so I thought. For no sooner did I belly up to the roulette table than I spied a red, digital sign proclaiming the following:

	MIN	MAX
Inside	$10	$25
Outside	$10	$500

And so my fantasy of throwing down a crisp hundred-dollar bill on a single inside bet was shown to be just that—a fantasy. That wasn't surprising, really. After all, given the odds of roulette, such a bet, if the number hit, would cost the house something on the order of $3,700, and we all know that the house prefers not to lose that kind of money. The best I could do, given the house rules, was to put $25 on four different inside numbers, and hope one of them turned up. If one did, the payout would still be something like $925, and yet, as I stood before the table doing all this math in my head, the idea of betting even $25 began to feel unthinkable.

Maybe that's why I've never been a gambler, I thought bleakly. *Maybe I lack whatever it is that gamblers have or are plagued by. Maybe if I had been one of those nineteenth-century trail drivers, I'd have been left behind to look after the herd while my fellow cowboys headed into town to raise hell . . .*

While I entertained these thoughts, one of the gamblers at the table, a fifty-something man in designer jeans and a cowboy hat, tossed a hundred-dollar bill at the croupier and waited to receive a stack of lavender-colored chips in return. The chips lasted all of four bets, whereupon the cowboy bought in again with a second hundred-dollar bill. These chips, too, were quickly lost.

About this time, Alyssa showed up at my elbow. "I found a couple of things I want to show you in the gift shop," she said. "Have you placed any bets?"

"No," I admitted. "Not yet."

"Well, what are you waiting for?"

As she said this, the man in the cowboy hat vacated his seat, and I took a twenty-dollar bill from my wallet and sat down at his place at the table. I felt suddenly nervous and out of place, an interloper in a world where I didn't belong. However, the other players at the table all nodded to me, friendly in a way I didn't expect them to be, and after the current round of betting ended, the croupier, a college-age kid with red hair and bad skin, took my money and slid twenty brown chips, each with the words BOOT HILL CASINO ROULETTE A emblazoned on them, across the green felt to me.

"Bets, please."

Turning to Alyssa, I whispered, "I'm going to put five chips on red and five on odd and one on number twenty-five."

"Put it on twenty-three," she answered, kneading my shoulders. "That's my lucky number."

"Twenty-three it is," I said dramatically, placing the bet.

We sat watching as the ball jumped around on the wheel before landing squarely on twenty-three red.

"We won!" I shouted, turning to Alyssa. "Can you believe it? We won!"

"I told you that was my lucky number," Alyssa said, winking at me.

A giddy feeling washed over me, followed by a shot of pure adrenaline, and I understood all at once what the thrill of the casino was all about, why those tired trail hands would bring their entire summer's pay into town and lay it on a single roll of the dice. It was about achieving just this feeling, using it to erase all of the hours of tedium that had gone into earning the money in the first place. But at the same time, I had too much respect for the whole idea of work to countenance either the throwing away of good money or the earning of it on something as unpredictable as a spinning wheel. Already I knew I was more or less done betting for the night. I had felt the essential thrill, so why go any further?

However, another surprise remained. For as the croupier pushed a stack of fifty-odd chips across the table at me, he smiled and, pointing to the red digital chart of minimum and maximum bets, said in an even voice, "I didn't notice before, but you bet five dollars each on two outside bets and just one dollar on your inside bet. The table minimum is ten dollars, inside or outside bet."

"Oh," I said, laughing nervously. "I forgot! I'm sorry!"

"Don't worry about it," the croupier answered, adding— and how I wish he hadn't!—"Just think what you'd have won if you played by the rules."

And so I did think about it, even as I mechanically put ten dollars on odd and lost and then picked up what remained of my winnings, thirty dollars all told, and carried the chips to the bank to cash them in, using the money to buy a series of cheesy gifts for friends and neighbors back home in Indiana.

"I should have bet the whole twenty dollars on twenty-three red," I whined to Alyssa. "The payout would have been, what, eight hundred dollars?"

"Yeah, but that's not who you are," she answered. "If you were that guy, you'd be back at that table right now, losing every dime you carried in here, and then some."

"You're probably right about that," I conceded. "There's probably no hope for me after all."

At the doors to the casino, I paused one last time to look up at the photomural of nineteenth-century cowboys. The men in the picture no longer looked so young to me. Instead, they seemed weathered and experienced, as if they already knew what I was just beginning to learn—about them, myself, and the awful, beautiful place we had both inhabited in our separate ways.

Outside, I paused yet again, this time to look up at the stars littering the night sky and to feel the harsh prairie wind whipping across the parking lot, throbbing the Stars and Stripes on its impossibly tall pole. How much harm could a couple of buildings do, anyhow, to something as big and bold as the plains? Hell, I could take my shoes off right now and walk from the parking lot, across the highway and the grassy ditch beyond, to that place where the American Legion pool, beacon of my childhood, once stood, and along the way I'd still be sure to encounter at least one sticker patch, and maybe a cow patty, too.

Maybe that's what the old-time cowboys felt, as well, leaving Dodge on their broken-down ponies, with their hundred-dollar hangovers and their empty pockets, to rejoin the herds of longhorns grazing the Big Basin south of town.

Spectacle is great and all, gambling and booze are great, but thank God for the stars, thank God for the land beneath the stars, thank God for the animals that defecate upon the land beneath the stars, so that man, in his infinite wisdom—and infinite folly—can step in it. Thank God thank God thank God . . .